THE WAY TO OUTDO ENGLAND WITHOUT FIGHTING HER.

LETTERS

TO THE

Hon. SCHUYLER COLFAX,

Speaker of the House of Representatives,

ON THE PAPER, THE IRON, THE FARMER'S, THE RAILROAD, AND THE CURRENCY QUESTIONS.

BY

HENRY C. CAREY,

AUTHOR OF "PRINCIPLES OF SOCIAL SCIENCE," ETC. ETC.

PHILADELPHIA:
HENRY CAREY BAIRD,
INDUSTRIAL PUBLISHER,
406 Walnut Street.
1865.

COLLINS, PRINTER, 705 JAYNE ST.

CONTENTS.

THE PAPER QUESTION

LETTER FIRST.

DEAR SIR :—

The gentlemen connected with the press, publishers of books and newspapers, have been for two years past, and are yet, engaged in the performance of an act that, as it seems to me, closely resembles suicide; and it is because of my desire to open their eyes to the fact that it really *is* suicidal in its tendencies, that I venture to trouble you with the perusal of this letter. Throughout by far the larger portion of my life I was one among them, and although many years have elapsed since I ceased to be connected with the business of publication, the feeling of interest in those concerned in it has remained wholly unimpaired. It is, therefore, as an old friend, late a co-laborer with themselves—a fellow-citizen having no interest in the question except in common with all who are around him—that to you, and through you to them, I propose to speak, hoping that they may be disposed to reflect carefully on the views that will be presented, and confidently believing that they may be satisfied that their recent course of proceeding, however injurious it may be to the makers of paper, tends to the production of results utterly destructive to themselves.

Most naturally they are anxious that paper shall be cheap, and that their business may be large and profitable. So am I, well knowing, as I do, that it is to the universal development of intellect among our people that we now stand indebted for the fact that this Union has been maintained; and, that if we are to prosper in the future it is in the direction of a further and more complete development of the national mind that prosperity must be sought. To that end, books and newspapers must be placed within the reach of all, old and young, poor and rich, black and white.

Thus fully agreeing with them in the result at which we should desire to arrive, I propose now to ask both you and them to look with me to the measures by which it may be attained. To that end, allow me now to ask the question—What are the circumstances under which commodities of all kinds tend to become cheaper? Is it not when and where there is *competition for their sale?* What, on the contrary, are those in which they tend to become dearer? Is it not when and where there is *competition for their purchase?* To these questions there can be but one reply, and that in the affirmative.

What, now, I would ask, has been the tendency of the action of our publishing friends throughout the last two years? Has it tended to promote the building of mills and the increase of competition for the sale of paper? As it seems to me, it has not. On the contrary, as I propose to show, it has been in a direction exactly the reverse of this. If so, are not, then, they themselves the authors of the grievances of which they now so much complain? That they are, I firmly believe, and equally firm is my belief that they may be satisfied that such has been the case. Should they be so, then may we once again see harmony established between two great interests, each of which is so directly interested in the prosperity of the other that it is, as I am very certain, entirely impossible to injure either one without at the same time inflicting serious injury on the other. Break down the cotton-spinners, and the weavers will soon cease to prosper. Break down the paper-makers, and the printers will soon see their hands deprived of employment, and their offices closed.

By the free-trade tariff of 1846, that tariff to which we are mainly indebted for all our present troubles, the duty on paper was fixed at 30 per cent. By the *ultra* free-trade tariff of 1857 it was reduced to 24 per cent.; but as the duties on all the raw materials of the manufacture—soda ash, bleaching powders, rosin, felting, wire-cloths, &c. &c.—were correspondingly reduced, the change was really unimportant.

By the Act of 1861 paper was restored to the place assigned to it by the free-traders of 1846, being subjected to a duty of 30 per cent. The duties on raw materials were, however, largely increased, and in some cases more than trebled. Alum was carried up from 15 to 50 cents per 100 pounds, while bleaching powders were raised from 4 cents to 30, and soda ash from 4 to 50. Such having been the case, it may be regarded as certain that this most important manufacture had not been allowed to profit in even the slightest degree of the adoption by the Chicago Convention of *Protection to Domestic Industry* as a part of the platform of principles upon which the party was to stand for all the future. Of all the various industries of the country, it was, as I believe, the only one that was thus excluded, and yet, in all my intercourse since that date with gentlemen interested therein, I have never heard the exclusion made the subject of complaint. It was wrong, nevertheless.

At the date of the passage of that act the country had for several months been so greatly agitated by the secession movement that trade of all kinds was nearly at a stand. Competition for the purchase of paper had no existence; but the competition for its sale had so greatly grown that the market price was below its actual cost, while every foreign product used in the manufacture came to the manufacturer burthened with the increase of duty to which I have referred. This state of things continued throughout the whole of the year 1861, and the change was afterwards but very slight until towards the close of the summer of 1862. As a consequence of this long-continued pressure upon their resources many paper-makers became bankrupt, while throughout the country mills were everywhere idle and unproductive.

Such was the state of things when, on the first of July, 1862, Congress passed a law imposing a tax of 3 per cent. upon all the paper made in the country, and a further tax of 3 per cent. upon the incomes of all concerned in the making of it. A fortnight later, with a view to retaining for the domestic manufacturer the place, in reference to the foreign one, he previously had occupied, the duties on imports were increased, and paper was raised from 30 to 35 per cent. Thus far, therefore, the paper-maker continued to be excluded from all share in the advantages derived by other branches of manufacture from the great change of public opinion that had been manifested by the most enthusiastic adoption of the protectionist plank of the Chicago Platform.

Shortly after this the commerce of the country began most rapidly to revive, and with that revival came a great increase in the demand for paper. Then, and not until then, the paper consuming world began to appreciate the effect on the supply of rags resulting from the closing of Southern ports against the export of cotton. Cotton goods were scarce and dear, and all were endeavoring to avoid their purchase. The old shirt continued to be used when, under other circumstances, it would have gone to the paper-mill. Cotton waste was no longer to be obtained. Linens, too, had greatly risen. The domestic supply of raw material was wholly insufficient for meeting the now rapidly increasing demand, and prices rose with a rapidity proportionate to the alarm excited among the paper-makers in reference to the power to keep their mills at work, and among the consumers in reference to obtaining at any price a full supply of paper. Abroad, and for the same reason, prices had advanced, and to the augmentation thus produced was here to be added the premium on the gold with which to pay for the rags that might be thence obtained. To all this was further to be added the premium on the gold required to pay for the alum, the bleaching powder, the felting, the wire-cloth, and other commodities needed in the manufacture. Coal, of which there is required, as I am assured, pound for pound of paper, and even more, had much increased in price, while labor also had much advanced.

As a consequence of all these things the price of paper went rapidly up, and to those manufacturers who had succeeded in stemming the tide in the past two years there opened up a prospect of obtaining profits that might perhaps indemnify them for the losses that had been sustained. *This was precisely the state of things that should have been desired by the paper consumers, being that which was needed for reopening mills that had been closed, for promoting the building of new ones, for utilizing new materials, and for thus stimulating all to increased competition for the sale of paper.* Instead of looking at it in this light, they at once raised a cry of monopoly which was persevered in throughout the whole of the ensuing session of Congress, until, just at its close, the duty on paper was, *most unfortunately for those who asked it,* reduced to 20 per cent. More unfortunate by far would they have been had they fully succeeded, as they had asked an entire repeal of the duty, the effect of which must have been that of closing nearly every printing paper-mill in the country, and placing them entirely at the mercy of European manufacturers. Had they then succeeded, they would this day be as clamorous for the re-establishment of protection as they now are for an extension of the free trade system.

The duty on printing paper had now been reduced to one-sixth less than that at which it had been fixed by the ultra free trade tariff of 1857. In the mean time raw materials of every kind had been heavily taxed—paper itself had been taxed three per cent.—and the incomes of the unfortunate people who had thus been placed under the ban had been subjected to a tax of the same amount. Making allowance for all these things the real duty, to which they could at all look for protection, was not even one-half as great as it had been under that ultra free trade tariff to which we had been so largely indebted for the crisis of 1857 and for the ruin of so large a proportion of the most useful portion of our people.

Why, however, it may be asked, should *any* protection yet be needed? For an answer to this question I would beg, my dear sir, to refer you to the following passage from a Report made but a few years since to the British Parliament, every word of which is as fully applicable to the trades in paper, glass, cloth, and chemicals, as it is to that in iron:—

"The laboring classes generally, in the manufacturing districts of this country and especially in the iron and coal districts, are very little aware of the extent to which they are often indebted for their being employed at all to the immense *losses* which their employers voluntarily incur in bad times, in order *to destroy foreign competition, and to gain and keep possession of foreign markets.* Authentic instances are well known of employers having in such times carried on their works at a loss amounting in the aggregate to three or four hundred thousand pounds in the course of three or four years. If the efforts of those who encourage the combinations to restrict the amount of labor and to produce strikes were to be successful for any length of time, the great accumulations of capital could no longer be made *which enable a few of the most wealthy capitalists to overwhelm all foreign competition in times of great depression*, and thus to clear the way for the *whole trade* to step in when prices revive, and to carry on a great business before *foreign* capital can again accumulate to such an extent as to be able to establish a competition in prices with any chance of success. *The large capitals of this country are the great instruments of warfare against the competing capital of foreign countries*, and are *the most essential* instruments now remaining by which our manufacturing supremacy can be maintained; the other elements—cheap labor, abundance of raw material, means of communication, and skilled labor—being rapidly in process of being equalized."

The "great capitalists" here referred to are steadily creating monopolies for themselves in Great Britain herself as well as in foreign countries. When they supply foreign markets at less than cost they do the same at home, and thus ruin the small capitalists around them. Therefore is it that the iron manufacture and the ownership of mines are becoming from year to year more and more concentrated in the hands of a few wealthy men, who hold quarterly meetings at which they decide how much coal shall be mined, how much iron is to be made, and at what prices the two may be sold. It is in the hands of just such men, immediate neighbors of those above described, that the consumers of paper are now laboring to place the control of the supply of the commodity they so much need. Whether or not it is in that direction they are to look for that increase in the competition for its sale without which there can be no reduction of prices, I leave it to you and them to judge.

Notwithstanding the reduction of duty that had taken place, some few mills, as I am informed, were built in 1863. Others that had been closed were once again opened, and had the paper consumers been willing to let the matter rest where it had been placed by the act of March of that year, it is quite certain that the number of new ones would by this time have been so largely increased as to set at rest for all future time the question of supply. Had they so acquiesced, the competition at the present moment would, as I am well satisfied, be for the *sale*, and not for the *purchase* of paper. The tendency of prices would have then been downwards.

That, however, they did not do. On the contrary, agitation for the total repeal of the duty was kept steadily up, with no effect so far as regarded the action of Congress, but with, *to themselves*, the most injurious effect upon the public mind. Up to that time there had still existed a strong belief that the necessity for revenue, and the growing conviction that it had been to protection we had been indebted for the power to pass through the great crisis of the rebellion, must suffice for making permanent the system that had been so well established. Now, however, it came to be seen that there was really no security, and that any one who should build a paper-mill would do it with the sword of Damocles always suspended over his head, and ever ready to fall. How this has probably affected the minds of hundreds of persons may be judged from a fact that is of my own knowledge. A year since, one of my friends, a man of large means, was preparing to make a great addition to the paper-producing power of the country, but of this idea he was entirely cured by the action of the paper consumers during the late session of Congress, and his works remain unbuilt. What is true of him cannot fail to have been equally so of very many others similarly situated. Capital has been abundant, but it has not gone in the direction of mills for making printing-paper, nor will it do so while the agitation shall be continued. Capitalists are timid people. They see that the paper consumers seem resolved upon killing the paper producers, and are not yet quite ready to bow their heads to the axe.

The agitation has now recommenced, and with redoubled force. It may be that our friends who are so anxious for cheap paper will this time succeed. If they shall do so, it is my prediction, and I pray you to note it, that, ere long, they will regret it far more bitterly than will the men whose mills will then have been closed, and who will then have been ruined. For a very brief period they may have paper cheaper from abroad; but as by degrees the weaker manufacturers are driven out of the business, the demand on Europe will steadily grow, and with that growth there will be an increase of the European prices that will make their paper cost them more than now, and *that* increase will be a permanent one. Those few among ourselves who can afford to stand aloof until the work of destruction shall have been accomplished will then step in and divide with the European manufacturers the profits of the market. Quarterly meetings will then probably be held, at which it will be decided what is the price at which the consumers of paper will be permitted to obtain the supplies they need, and the latter will then discover that they have exchanged the rule of the quiet king Log for that of the active and energetic Stork, so well described by our old friend Æsop. Few of them will now, probably, be disposed to believe this, but they will realize its absolute truth should they this time be so unfortunate as to succeed in the work in which they are engaged. Unhappily for them, the damage will then have become irremediable.

To those who may doubt the correctness of the views thus presented, I beg to recommend a consideration of the following facts:—

Rags can be more cheaply brought to England, France, and Belgium than to these United States:

Labor is there abundant and cheap, while here it is scarce and dear:

The field for the employment of labor throughout the South and

West is likely to enlarge with such rapidity as to cause that scarcity and that dearness to continue for a long period of time:

Iron is cheaper abroad, and machinery may there be obtained at greatly lower cost:

Felting, bleaching powders, alum, and all other of the commodities used in making paper, can be obtained free of the duty they must pay on entering here:

Coal is cheaper, and steam is less costly:

Interest is there little more than half of what is paid by the American manufacturer; and—

There is there no excise duty of three per cent.

Such being a part only of the great differences between the two sides of the Atlantic, can any reasonable man, proprietor of a newspaper, doubt that the "great capitals" of Europe will at once be set to work *to crush out American competition for the sale of this great commodity*, an abundant and cheap supply of which is now more important than it has been at any period of our history? If any such there should prove to be, he would, as I think, only furnish new evidence of the perfect truth of the idea, that "whom the gods would destroy, they first make mad."

Were I owner of the *Tribune*, *Post*, or *Ledger*, and in that capacity invested with full power to act for our friends of the Associated Press, the change that is now asked for should not be made were the foreign manufacturers ready to pay into the treasury of that association, to be distributed *pro rata*, according to their interests, among the book and newspaper publishers of the country, *thirty millions of dollars*. Large as is this sum, I would reject it, and for the reason, that it would be no compensation for the damage to be done to the private interests of my associates, leaving wholly out of view those of the country at large.

In regard to these latter, I will only call your attention to the fact, that the day is close at hand when we shall have to provide literary food for sixty millions of people, and that if they are to be at all supplied it must be by means of measures that shall tend to enable small manufacturers to accumulate capital and enlarge their operations so as to increase the competition for the *sale* of paper; and not by means of a present agitation which alarms the great capitalist and prevents him from investing his means in this department of manufacture, to be followed by a British free-trade policy that cannot fail to bring with it utter ruin to all the smaller capitalists already engaged in it.

Ten years since there was a similar agitation for the abolition of duties on railroad iron. It lasted several years, and, as I believe, until the revulsion of 1857 had taught us the *advantages* of the British free-trade system. During all that time no one could be found hardy enough to build either a mill or a furnace. After the revulsion there was great depression, as a consequence of which the consumption of iron in 1860 was scarcely, if at all, greater than it had been a dozen years before, and yet the population had increased more than forty per cent. But for that agitation, we should to-day be producing *thrice* the quantity of iron that is now being consumed; we should be exporting instead of importing it; the demand for gold would be less; and our people would be saving annually on their purchases of that one commodity fifteen or twenty millions of dollars. Just so will it be with our publishing friends. Their agitation of the past three years has already thrown us back at least one year. Let them now succeed, and they will throw themselves back twenty years, for then no one can ever again have the smallest confidence in any change of system that may be made.

If paper-making is really very profitable, let them build mills and thus promote competition for the supply of the market. In this way they will serve themselves and their country too. The introduction of new materials to take the place of the now deficient cotton demands large investments of capital, but will in the end greatly lessen the cost of paper. Let *them* supply that capital. Pending the existing agitation others will certainly not do so.

Having thus shown what, as I think, they owe to themselves, I propose in another letter to show what are the privileges they enjoy, and what are the duties they owe to the community of which they are a part. In the mean time, allow me, my dear sir, to ask you to reflect for a moment on the moral of another well-known fable of Æsop, entitled "The Wind and the Sun." The more the former raged the more the traveller clung to his cloak, and the more closely he wrapped it around his limbs. Seeing this, Mr. Wind abandoned the effort, and made way for Mr. Sun, under the powerful influence of whose beams the cloak was quickly laid aside. Our friends have played the part of Wind for two years past, and with no other effect than that of raising the price of paper. Let them now take that of Sun—let them declare for a *permanent* peace—and there will be more mills built in the next twelve months than have been built in the past three years, or will be so in the next half century if the war is to be maintained.

Begging you now to excuse this trespass on your attention, and hoping that you may find in what I have written evidence of my sincere anxiety for the prosperity of the great publishing interests, I remain, my dear sir, with great regard and respect,

Yours, faithfully,

HENRY C. CAREY.

Hon. SCHUYLER COLFAX.

PHILADELPHIA, Dec. 24, 1864.

THE PAPER QUESTION.

LETTER SECOND.

Dear Sir:—

Hitherto, agitation in reference to the proposed repeal of the paper duty has been carried on through the public prints. Now, however, the course of operation seems to be entirely different, not an editorial line in reference to it having yet met my eyes, with the single exception of a brief article from the *Evening Post*, here given for the reason that always in the past it has been, and now is, my wish that our people should have the opportunity afforded them of seeing all that could be said on both sides of the great question of bringing the consumer to the side of the producer, and thus relieving the farmer from the oppressive tax of transportation to which he has so long been subjected. Had the *Post*, and its free trade brethren, followed the example, we might have been saved much of the loss and trouble of the past four years. The article referred to is as follows:—

The Paper Duty.—"The duty on printing paper was, we suppose, intended by those who laid it to produce revenue to the treasury. Its only effect, however, is to put money into the pockets of the American manufacturers. The duty is twenty per cent., *ad valorem;* this is payable in gold, and it has made importation impossible. It does this in the following way:—

"The manufacturers of printing paper here set their prices so as to leave no margin of certain profit to the importer who must pay a duty of twenty per cent., in gold, at the same time their profits enable them, if necessary, to undersell and drive out of the market with loss any one who should attempt to import.

"Printing paper sold for from nine to ten cents per pound before the war. It is sold for eight cents per pound in Europe at this time. But in this country publishers are forced to pay for newspaper from twenty-four to thirty cents. Take off the duty and it can be imported for from seventeen to eighteen cents per pound, currency; and at that price American manufacturers can still make and sell at a fair profit.

"A duty which yields no revenue is an absurdity. The present twenty per cent. duty upon paper is prohibitory, its only use is to take money out of the pockets of the public and put it into the pockets of a few already wealthy manufacturers. Even the government pays tribute, under present arrangements, to these capitalists for the immense quantity of paper it uses. The present Congress ought to remedy this wrong by repealing the duty on paper."

That what is here given as fact in regard to the cost of paper, and the profits of paper-making, is wholly incorrect might readily be shown, but I have no desire to annoy you with the examination of little figures. It is greatly to the interest of the publishers of both books and newspapers that the makers of paper should be so well paid as to enable those who are in the business to extend their works, while stimulating outside capitalists to employ their means in erecting new ones; and if I could be assured that all were really as herein stated, I should most heartily rejoice at it in the interest of the paper consumers. Let it be clearly shown that paper-mills can be securely relied upon to yield ten, twelve, or fifteen per cent. per annum, and we shall see more new ones commenced in the next twelve months than have been started in the last decade. Let the work of agitation be continued and there will not be even a single one; and that, too, even if it prove, session after session for the next ten years, to be wholly fruitless. The capitalist *will* not, with his eyes now fully opened, engage in a war with the Press. If, then, the monopoly here complained of be continued, our publishing friends will have only themselves to thank for it.

It is complained that the duty is prohibitory, and yet, making allowances for taxes imposed since 1860, the protection afforded is less than ten per cent. If, at such a moderate rate, the foreign traders of New York, admirable as they have always been in the manufacture of false invoices, cannot import paper, there can exist no shadow even of cause for complaint. As it seems to me the *Post* has proved rather too much.

What, however, are the privileges now enjoyed by that and other journals? Do *they* at all savor of prohibition? Let us inquire.

Five years since there were two branches of industry that were protected by means of absolute prohibition of foreign interference, the production of negro slaves, and that of newspapers. The Virginia planter, anxious as he might be for free trade in iron, could manufacture his corn into chattels for which he could obtain eight, or even ten times the price at which similar machines could be imported from abroad. Why was this? Because Congress had prohibited foreign competition, and thus preserved to him the control of the domestic market. That branch of manufacture having, however, been since abolished, there now remains but a single one that profits by prohibition, and must, in all future times, continue so to do—that one being the newspaper.

The *Post*, the *Tribune*, the *Ledger*, the *North American*, the *Transcript*, and the *Daily Advertiser*, cannot be produced abroad. Come what may—let us have war or peace, prosperity or adversity, free trade or protection—they must still be manufactured in New York, Philadelphia, and Boston. The control of the domestic market is thus secured to the domestic manufacturer, and by a law that can never be repealed; and *therefore is it that the consumer is supplied with information at less cost than in any country of the world.* So will it be with paper whenever the consumers shall have arrived at the conclusion that the law which has proved in their own cases so very true cannot fail to prove equally so in regard to the commodities in whose cheap production they are so deeply interested.

Not only have the proprietors of these and other journals a monopoly of the general market of the country, as against foreigners, but they have, each and all, their shares in a monopoly that is not to be interfered with even by the domestic capitalist. To start a new paper in New York, and to continue it long enough to secure the circulation without which advertising cannot be obtained, is a work that certainly cannot to-day be accomplished at a cost of $250,000. It might cost much more than this, and even then it might prove a failure. So clearly is this understood that the proprietors of existing journals now laugh to scorn the idea of danger from future interference.

Perfectly secure, then, against both foreign and domestic competition, those gentlemen are enabled to throw upon the public, all of the burthen of which they now so much complain, the former one cent paper being now sold for two, and the two cent one for four—the difference being nearly the whole cost of the paper that is used. A pound will give 18 sheets for the first and 10 or 12 for the second, and thus the *additional* charge is little less than twenty cents per pound. In many cases it exceeds 25 cents per pound. Such paper may now, as I am informed, readily be bought for from 20 to 23 cents.

Turning next to advertising, we find New York journalists profiting of their absolute monopoly by charging nearly as much for the insertion of a single line as formerly would have been charged for that of a whole square. Forty cents per line is, as I am told, the present charge of the *Herald*. In several of the weekly papers it is from $1 to $1.50 per line. Surely the persons who make such charges have little reason to complain of the present trivial duty upon the one great commodity they so much need.

Secured thus, now and forever, in the enjoyment of one of the greatest monopolies of the world, the selling price of interests in these journals is wonderfully great. Shares in several of them can be sold, as I understand, at the rate of from three to five hundred thousand dollars for the whole, the purchaser paying in addition as much as may be considered the fair value of an equivalent share of the machinery in use. Elsewhere larger sums would, as I understand, be demanded, and when we should reach the highest figure it would probably prove to be little short of $800,000.

Let this now be compared with the value of the property that is devoted to the production of printing paper, and then determine which of the parties to this suit it is that has most reason for complaint. There is not, as I am assured, and as I believe, a printing paper-mill in any of the Atlantic States that would sell for more than the actual cost of the buildings and machinery, while some, and even the best of them, may be had this day at much less than the actual cost. If the profits of such concerns are really as large as they are described by the *Post* to be, why do not the complainants purchase them and manufacture on their own account? For the simple reason that the making of printing paper, on an average of the last half century, has been one of the worst paid pursuits in which a man could be engaged. It would be difficult, as I believe, to find any one requiring as much intelligence and as much capital in which so few have acquired fortunes.

On some recent occasion I have seen a statement of the wonderful growth in prosperity of the *Post* itself, and unless I am greatly in error in regard to the figures therein given, the mere good-will of that paper, which has cost no man even a single shilling, would sell for more than all the buildings and machinery of the largest printing paper mill in the Union.

While presenting these facts I beg not to be regarded as at all complaining of the prosperity of journalists. The more they prosper the more shall I rejoice, but not the less shall I object to their complaining of a miserable little item of *protection*, while they are becoming rich by help of AN ABSOLUTE PROHIBITION established by nature herself, and not in any manner dependent on the caprices of Congress. The eagle suffers little birds to sing, and they, as I think, may well afford to permit the poor paper-makers to live and educate their children, even if they be not allowed to leave behind them any fortune.

What is true of journalists is almost equally so in regard to the publishers of books. In former times Worcester, Albany, Poughkeepsie, Baltimore, Washington, and Richmond, competed with Boston, New York, and Philadelphia, in this department of manufacture. Within these latter, too, there was a competition that made it very dangerous to fix a book at too high a price. Gradually, machinery took the place of the human hand, and with every such improvement the business of publication more and more centered itself in the three great cities, the reading public profiting, by means of cheap books, of all the changes that were made. The business grew, and with that growth came a division of employments; the various departments of literature obtaining each their special representatives. With every step in this direction there came a diminution of competition accompanied by a rise of price, the result now exhibiting itself in this fact, that books are rapidly attaining the enormous English prices. At no time, as I am informed, and as I believe, have profits been so large. If this is so, as it probably is, surely the men who make them may permit their slaves to live. They *must* do so if they would continue to live themselves. Close the American paper mills, and most of them *will* be closed if Congress shall sanction the commission of the suicidal act that is now proposed, and we shall not long continue to hear of 15, 20, 50, and even as high as 100,000 dollars a year as the profit realized by the publishers of a single magazine or a single newspaper.

The word *slave* has been used above, and most advisedly. Our people are divided into two great classes, those who can, and those who cannot, maintain direct commerce with the consumers of their products. The first constitute the privileged class vested with power to control at their discretion the movements of the second, these last "living, moving, and having their being" at the pleasure of their masters. The owner of the railroad fixes for himself the terms on which he will permit the coal producer, or the traveller, to use his road; and he adheres to his contract just so long as it suits him, and not an hour longer. He interprets the words of his charter to suit himself, well knowing that he is in the full enjoyment of a monopoly, and that he can set at defiance all efforts at resistance. It is through him, and him alone, that the railroad iron manufacturer draws his support from the public at large. He, therefore, may meet his fellow managers for the purpose of determining in secret conclave exactly to what extent it may be safe to grind the poor producers of wheat, cotton, coal, and iron; but let the iron producers hold a meeting and at once a cry is raised of combination to keep up prices and thus to rob the public, the aid of Congress being then at once invoked for the punishment of men who manifest such determination "to grind the faces of the poor."

The book publisher deals directly with the public, and he arranges his prices to suit himself. Through him it is that the printer and the binder deal with the world at large. As a necessary consequence of this, the middleman builds a palace in which to transact his business, and another in which to live; while the poor printer, or the yet poorer binder, is forced to rejoice in the fact that he yet obtains the means with which to educate his children and to clothe himself.

The maker of writing paper deals, if he pleases, directly with the outside world. He may open a shop when and where it suits him, as a consequence of which the stationer respects his rights. He, therefore, has been permitted to retain all the protection granted to him by the tariffs of '61 and '62.

Widely different is the condition of the maker of printing paper, for to enable him to maintain commerce with the world, he must have the aid of the publishers of books and newspapers. They are, therefore, his masters. If he and his fellow-slaves meet together to talk of their general interests, there is charge of "combination." The book is doubled in price, its publisher thus forcing the consumer to pay all his taxes, with the usual profits thereon to himself, he himself, meanwhile, denying the right of the paper-makers even to consult together on the propriety of adding to their prices the simple amount of their contributions for the support of Government.

The publisher of newspapers, secure in the enjoyment of his

monopoly, cares nothing about tariffs. The world may complain as it likes when he doubles, trebles, or even quadruples the charge for advertising, he well knowing that, like the collector of railroad tolls, or steamboat fares, he has but to ring his bell to have them all "step up to the captain's office and settle." Of all the privileged classes of the country he is the man who is most secure. If his hands turn out he calls on the public for aid in his contests with them, and forthwith, as has recently been seen in Boston, men of all classes come to his assistance. If, however, the poor paper-maker be found seeking to obtain some small compensation for a year or two of loss, he flies to Congress, talks of "combination prices," and insists that, while he himself enjoys entire and absolute protection in the domestic market, his unhappy dependent shall be at once deprived of the little that has yet been left. Fully secured in the enjoyment of his privileges, he rejoices when the world is told that the value of the mere good-will of his establishment counts by hundreds of thousands of dollars, while denouncing as a monopolist the poor serf who furnishes him with paper, and who would gladly sell to him at cost, the mill in which it is accustomed to be made. He is, however, quite too wise to purchase.

A story is told of an old *contraband* that may be worth repeating here, as it tolerably well illustrates the positions of the parties. Corn being scarce while he had a large litter of pigs to feed, he was heard calling on Heaven to send the time when corn should be at a shilling a bushel and pork at two shillings a pound. The governing class having now put up their own pork to two shillings, are most anxious to reduce the price of their neighbor's corn. The road, however, in which they are travelling leads in another direction, as they will be sure to find if they shall continue on it until they reach its end.

Throughout the whole range of this highly privileged order of beings there is none that has more steadily than the *Post* talked of freedom; none that has more persistently cracked the whip over the dependent class to which I have referred, producers of fuel, machinery, and paper—hewers of its wood and drawers of its water—the men without whose services it could not live itself for even another hour. That such should continue to be the case now that the Government has become dependent for its existence on the internal revenue is greatly to be regretted, and I cannot but hope that at no distant time the editors of this journal may come to see that it is in efficient protection we are to find the true and only road towards freedom of trade and freedom for man.

Before closing this letter allow me to ask your attention to the following paragraph telegraphed last week, by the Associated Press as I suppose, to numerous Northern journals :—

"COST OF PAPER.—The Superintendent of Public Printing reports to the Ways and Means Committee a deficit of five hundred thousand dollars in the appropriation for the purchase of paper. When the last appropriation was made, the contract price for book paper was eighteen cents a pound. Mr. Defrees's estimate was upon that basis. Congress subsequently imposed a heavy tariff on paper. Paper-makers rushed into a combination and raised the price of paper to the amount of the duty. The Government is now paying from thirty-one to thirty-seven cents per pound for what previously cost eighteen to twenty-one cents. The Treasury is receiving no revenue from paper, because none is imported, the duty being prohibitory."

Allow me now, my dear sir, to ask you to answer to yourself if the manufacture of statements such as these does not furnish evidence of conscious weakness on the part of those by whom they have been written. The man who made this paragraph well knew that the rise of which he spoke had been mainly due to the fact that a severe drought had, during several months, diminished by one-half the producing power of a large portion of the Northern paper-mills, but of this he has said not even a single word. He knew, too, that so far from Congress having "imposed a heavy tariff on paper," the last Acts of that body relating to this branch of manufacture had been the increase of taxes on domestic products, and the reduction, by nearly one-half, of the duties on foreign ones. The article is throughout utterly inaccurate, yet is it given to the world in the columns of journals edited and published by gentlemen who would feel themselves much aggrieved were we, in regard to private matters, to question their character for strict veracity. It is, however, but a repetition of the story of *The Wolf and the Lamb*, so well presented to us by our old friend Æsop. Determined to crush out his poor slave the master holds him responsible for all the accidents that have, in the last few months, diminished the supply, while adding to his own charge as much as covers *nearly the whole cost of the paper that is used.*

In presenting these views of a great question *that has now, as I think, to be definitively settled,* I am animated by no feeling of unkindness towards any of the interests to which reference has been made. What I do desire is to awaken all to a clear conception of their mutual dependence. When that conception shall have been fully reached, but not till then, a settlement of all the difficulties may be made on terms that should be satisfactory to all, and certainly would be advantageous to both the people and the government. The proclamation of emancipation did much towards bringing about the entire extinction of negro slavery throughout the continent, but it was not until the 8th of November last that the people affixed to it the Great Seal of the Republic. The Chicago proclamation of *emancipation for the white slaves of the North by means of efficient protection* was but the preparation for that great measure. The Great Seal had yet to be affixed, and the time has now arrived for doing it.

What is the manner in which this vitally important result is to be attained I propose to show in another letter, first, however, noticing the suggestions of the *Post* in reference to the very important question of revenue.

Meanwhile, I pray you, my dear sir, to accept the assurance of the sincere regard and respect with which I remain,

Yours, faithfully,

HENRY C. CAREY.

Hon. Schuyler Colfax.

Philadelphia, Dec. 26, 1864.

THE PAPER QUESTION.

LETTER THIRD.

DEAR SIR:—

Among the characters personated by the elder Matthews, in his admirable monologues, was one of an old angler who was bitterly hostile to the introduction of steam navigation on the ground that steamers "frightened the fish." Nearly akin to this, in its philosophy, was the idea of Mr. Walker, suggested in one of his Reports, that protection was injurious to the nation, and for the reason, that as domestic competition grew, prices declined with corresponding decrease of importation and of customs revenue. In his eyes the real saving of millions by the people was no sufficient offset to the apparent loss of thousands by the Federal Government. The loss had no real existence, the demand for sugar, tea, coffee, and a thousand other articles having always grown with a rapidity proportioned to that of the decline in the price of pins, needles, knives, and cotton. Following in the same direction the *Post*, participant in one of the most profitable monopolies of the world, assures its readers that "a duty which yields no revenue is an absurdity"—that it is "prohibitory"—that "it takes money out of the pockets of the public and puts it into the pockets of a few wealthy manufacturers," and that "Congress ought to remedy the wrong by repealing the duty on paper." Not a word, however, does it say about that natural prohibition which secures to its own proprietors the control of the domestic market for news, and gives to the mere *good-will* attached to its name a money value greater, probably, than that of any paper-mill in the Union, with all the land, the buildings, and the machinery of which it is composed.

Nominally, the duty on printing paper is 20 per cent.; really, it may perhaps be 15, but is more likely to be only 12½. Admitting, however, that the foreigner pays into the treasury 15 per cent., let us now compare that with what we know to be contributed for the support of Government by the domestic manufacturer, and thus enable ourselves to judge of the expediency of moving in the direction indicated by the *Post.*

The latter pays, in direct tax, three per cent. of the market value of his products. This was paid, in the last fiscal year, upon more than $22,000,000, and the amount received by the treasury, from all descriptions of paper, was $663,447. All experience shows that taxes become more productive as assessors come more and more to understand their duties, and there is therefore good reason for supposing that the yield will, in the present fiscal year, be much increased. To this let us now add the tax on incomes, late three per cent., but now five, to be paid by "already wealthy manufacturers," who would gladly accept, at the hands of the certainly wealthy proprietors of the *Post*, cost for all their works. Next, add the taxes on all the steam, bricks, lumber, and iron required for the erection of buildings, or for keeping them in repair. Further, add the amount paid as duties on soda ash, bleaching powders, alum, felting, and other commodities used in the manufacture. Again, let us add the tax on coal, of which it requires, even where water-power is used, more than pound for pound of paper, and much more when steam-power is required. Putting all these now together we shall probably reach ten per cent., giving a sum exceeding two millions of dollars as the direct contribution of this single branch of manufacture towards the payment of our troops, and the discharge of interest on our debt. This large sum it is that the treasury is required to relinquish in order that the *Post* may, free of all such charges, buy its paper in Belgium, France, or England.

The sacrifice thus far demanded by our publishing friends would appear to be quite large, and yet it is but a portion of that which really is required. The number of persons employed in the paper manufacture is stated at not less than 50,000. Putting their wages at an average of only $5 a week, we have $13,000,000. Of this, in the form of taxes on tea, coffee, sugar, &c. &c., there goes into the treasury probably $1,000,000, and thus do we obtain a total of $3,000,000 that we must relinquish in order that the British and Belgium manufacturer may be enabled to expel from our mills this large and interesting portion of our population.

We may be told, however, that these poor people, if driven from the mills, will find other employment. What is likely to be the nature of that employment may perhaps be inferred from the following extract from a circular issued by one of the charitable associations of New York, bearing date a year and a half previous to the occurrence of the great free-trade crisis of 1857 :—

"Up to the present, the Association has relieved 6,922 families, containing 26,896 persons, *many of whom are families of unemployed mechanics* and widows with dependent children, who cannot subsist without aid. As the season advances the destitution will increase. Last winter it was thrice as great in January as in December, and did not reach its height until the close of February."

It is in this state of things that immigration tends to die away, and here we find another of those sacrifices that we must make in order that our publishing friends may be enabled to buy their neighbor's corn cheap while selling their own pork at monopoly prices. What are the circumstances under which immigration grows, and what those under which it declines, I propose now to show, believing a full understanding of them to be essential to a proper understanding of the tendencies of the movements now in progress.

The first tariff really protective of the farmer in his efforts for drawing the consumer to his side, thereby relieving him from the oppressive tax of transportation, and from the slavery incident to a dependence on foreign markets, was enacted in the year 1828, and began, as we may reasonably suppose, to make itself in some degree effective in 1830. In the decade prior to this latter year the total immigration had amounted to 120,000, giving an annual average of but 12,000. Protection making demand for labor with large increase of wages, the effect soon exhibited itself in a larger import of persons who had that commodity to sell, and the immigration of 1830 amounted to 27,000. In the four following years it went steadily up until, in 1834, it had reached 65,000.

By the Compromise tariff of 1833 it was provided that protection should be gradually diminished until, in 1842, the country should be replaced under a free trade despotism more complete by far than that which had existed prior to 1828. As a consequence of this, factories and furnaces ceased to be built, and the whole energies of the country were given to the construction of roads and canals, by means of which its products were to be enabled to reach the distant market. Its credit stood very high, the few years of the protective policy that had just then closed having enabled the government, in 1835, to pay off the last remaining portion of the public debt.

Loans were therefore readily negotiated in Europe, and for a brief period there existed a glare of prosperity well calculated to deceive those who could not appreciate the great fact, that the raising of raw products for distant markets tended to exhaustion of the soil, and was the proper work of the barbarian and the slave, and of those alone.

Three years only of the free trade system were required for producing the crisis of 1837, to be followed by the crash of 1839, and the almost universal bankruptcy of 1841 and 1842. During all this period immigration was of the most fitful kind, rising as moneys were borrowed abroad and roads were commenced at home, and falling as bankruptcies grew in number and half finished roads were left to go to ruin; but its annual average, notwithstanding the large extension of internal communications, scarcely exceeded the figure it had so rapidly attained in 1834, having been only 67,500.

The two first years of the highly protective tariff of 1842, gave an average of 81,000. Thenceforward immigration grew steadily until, in 1847 and 1848, it reached an average of 234,000, having thus almost trebled in that brief period. The effects of the free trade tariff of 1846 were just then beginning to be felt. Mines thenceforward ceased to be opened, and mills and furnaces ceased to be built. Labor was everywhere in excess of the demand, and immigration must rapidly have declined had not the discovery of Californian gold opened up a new branch of industry, calculated to operate largely on the minds of the miners and laborers of the world at large.

The gold received at the United States Mint for coinage, in 1849, amounted to $9,000,000, or more than had been received from all the world in the six years from 1837–42. In 1850 it reached $32,000,000, and in the following year it rose to $62,000,000. Immigration grew therefore rapidly, giving for the four years succeeding 1850 the following figures:—

1851 . . .	408,000	1853 . . .	401,000
1852 . . .	397,000	1854 . . .	460,000

Up to that time gold washing had been very profitable, but thenceforward it became from year to year more clearly obvious that a continuance of the gold supply was to be obtained only by means tending to render the laborer a mere machine to be used by the capitalist. The demand for men for California was therefore at an end, while that for the Atlantic States and the Mississippi Valley tended steadily to decline, because of the constantly growing excess in the supply of labor consequent upon the closing of mills, furnaces, factories, and machine shops. Hence it is that the succeeding years furnish us with the following diminished quantities :—

1855 . . .	230,000	1858	149,000
1856 . . .	224,000	1859	155,000
1857 . . .	271,000	1860	179,000

Small as are these figures, they would probably be diminished not less than 25 per cent. were we furnished with those that would be required for enabling us to ascertain the numbers of the disappointed who returned to Europe, or who left California to seek fortune in the more attractive gold deposits of Australia. At no period in the history of the country, as I believe, had the average rate of interest been so high as in the four years above referred to. At none had there been so great a tendency to decline in the reward of the laborer, and hence it was that immigration so rapidly declined.

The Southern rebellion having at length emancipated the North, protection was re-established by means of that Morrill tariff, so much denounced by the *Post;* that tariff to which we are indebted for the fact that all Europe is now so largely engaged in manufacturing machines of the most valuable kind, to be *presented* to us, in free gift, by those who make them. While compelling us to give gold for silks and cottons, the nations beyond the Atlantic are willing to give us men and women who can not only spin and weave, but who can make the machinery by means of which spinning and weaving may be done, and at the same time reproduce themselves. Of all foreign products, they are the most costly and most valuable, and they are to be obtained at the cheap price of the steady pursuit of a policy that will make a market close to the farmer's door, and thus treble the price of his land.

Under the Morrill tariff system, immigration in the last year, as shown in the records of the State Department, rose to 200,000, but to this must be added at least 50,000 who had been attracted from the British provinces, and of whom no record had been kept. In the present year there has been a large increase, and from both those sources; but we are not yet in possession of all the figures required for enabling us to give them with any approach to accuracy. Let us, however, go ahead with the protective system; let us manifest a fixed determination to bring the consumer close to the producer's door; and the day will not then be far distant when the numbers of foreigners seeking to take their place among us will be as much in excess of those of present years as were those of 1847 in excess of 1842.

Protection looks to producing competition for the *purchase* of labor, and for that of the rude products of the farm, and therefore does it tend in the direction of freedom. British free trade seeks to produce competition for the *sale* of both, and therefore is it that, throughout the present war, it has shown itself the faithful ally of the men who teach that slavery is the natural condition of the laboring man, whether black or white.

The more numerous the mills and furnaces the greater is the competition for the *sale* of paper, cloth, and iron, the greater is the tendency towards reduction of their prices, the greater is the competition for the *purchase* of labor, and the larger, as has here been shown, is the number of persons who come here to aid, by the consumption of sugar, tea, coffee, paper, cloth, and other commodities, in the maintenance of that great domestic revenue to which the Government must in future look for payment of its annual expenses, and for the ultimate redemption of its bonds. Half a million of such persons coming here, and earning on an average but five dollars a week, would receive an aggregate of wages amounting to $130,000,000. Ten per cent. paid on this to the Government would be $13,000,000. The *Post* would shut them out, it being an "absurdity" to maintain on the statute book a law imposing a duty whose only effect was that of causing foreign workmen to come here and labor in our mills, eating our own food and wearing our own cloth, when men could be found abroad who *might, perhaps*, supply paper, iron, and cloth more cheaply, but certainly would apply their wages to the purchase of the food of Germany, France, or England, while contributing annually more than a tithe of their earnings to the support of foreign governments. The more such people came here, the smaller would be the tax of transportation paid by the farmer, the greater would be the value of his land, and the larger would be the amount of his contributions for the support of both the State and Federal Governments. How many *would* come under the system now advocated by the *Post*?

But a few years since that journal told its readers that "it would be better for all of them [the sewing women] in the long run, to reduce wages to the famine point, so as to force all who had sufficient strength into other employments." Now, it would close the door to them in reference to that "other" one which makes demand for so much female labor, the manufacture of paper. Seeking some new "employment" they might, perhaps, find it in bleaching shops, where they would be required to compete, wholly unprotected, with British men, women, and children, who are, as shown in Parliament, obliged to work 16 to 20 hours per day, and under a temperature so high that not unfrequently "the nails in the floors become heated and blister the feet of those employed in the rooms, usually called *wasting shops*, because of the extraordinary cost of life of which they are the cause." How much could our people, subjected to competition with such as here described, contribute towards the hundreds of millions of internal revenue of which we now stand so much in need? Not very much, as I think.

It is time that those gentlemen should awaken to the fact that there is a harmony in all the real and permanent interests of the various portions of society—the paper maker and the publisher—the farmer and his customers—the people and their government. When they shall do so they will, as I think, arrive at a proper comprehension of the present "absurdity" of admitting foreign paper at a duty of less, probably, than a sixth of its real value, and the still greater one of freeing the foreign manufacturer from all contributions for the support of government, while taxing our own to the extent of probably ten per cent.

At the moment of writing this I find in one of our city journals a paragraph, copied from the *Post*, denouncing in regard to *matches* the precise policy it has itself so steadily advocated as that required to be pursued in reference to *paper*. It is as follows:—

"Those (matches) made in the country are taxed, by stamps, over two hundred per cent. on the cost of manufacture. But at the same session a tariff act has been passed imposing a duty, quite nominal in comparison, on foreign matches. Now, Mr. Stevens's act expressly provides, that (section 169) when any imported articles requiring stamps shall be sold 'in the original and unbroken packages' in which they were packed by the manufacturer, no penalty whatever shall be incurred by selling them without stamps! Of course, manufacturers in Canada and Europe have only to pack their goods in one or a few boxes, for family use, and they save the tax. Match factories were at once removed into Canada, and fortunes have been made in five months' recess of Congress by simply adopting the means which our law took pains to provide for defeating its own objects and ruining our own manufacturers."

If it is wrong to "ruin our own manufacturers" by taxing their matches while admitting those of Canada duty free, can it be right to tax home-made paper while admitting free that furnished by the great capitalists of Europe? It seems to me that it cannot, but I shall be glad to hear the argument of the *Post* in its defence. There will, as I think, be more consistency in the movements of that journal when it shall have arrived at the conclusion that protection is the true and only road towards perfect freedom of trade.

In my next I propose to show what are, as they appear to me, the duties of all of us who desire to see the Government sustained not only throughout the war, but after peace shall again have visited our land, meanwhile remaining, my dear sir,

Most respectfully yours,

HENRY C. CAREY.

Hon. SCHUYLER COLFAX.

PHILADELPHIA, December 29, 1864.

THE PAPER QUESTION.

LETTER FOURTH.

Dear Sir:—

A few months since a bank of the New York Canal was swept away for an extent of many miles, as a consequence of which navigation upon that work was suspended, as I think, during several weeks. The disaster was at the time attributed to the operations of an active and industrious rat who had burrowed into the canal, thus making way for a column of water to pass in the direction from which he had come. At first very small, it rapidly increased in size and force, and finally produced the disaster to which I have referred.

Precisely such an operation as this it is that is now going on in reference to the question of protection to the farmer in his efforts for drawing the consumer to his side, and thus relieving him from the present terrific tax of transportation. The first rat-hole was made in March, '63, when the paper-makers, after having been subjected to an infinity of taxes, were deprived of all the protection, little as it was, that had been granted to them by the tariff of '61. The second was made at the last session of Congress, when the taxes on home-made iron were almost doubled, while the duty on railroad iron was largely diminished. The hole made in '63 is now to be widened by means of the total repeal of the duty on paper. That accomplished, the opponents of the Government will find themselves emboldened to new efforts, and day by day we shall see the rat-holes increase in number and in size, until at length the whole work will be swept away, and with it all chance of any permanent maintenance of the Union, or of any future payment of its debts.

The managers of the great combination that is now engaged in the performance of a work regarded by the British people as so essential to their future greatness—the making of the rat-holes to which I have referred—are to be found among the men who have furnished the ships and men by which the blockade of Southern ports has been evaded; those who have fitted out the pirate ships by means of which the flag of the Union has been almost entirely driven from the ocean; those who have, in and out of Parliament, systematically endeavored to destroy the credit of our Government while vilifying our people; and those who see in the continued maintenance of the Union the writing on the wall which warns them that the day is close at hand when the people of Europe will demand for themselves that exercise of the privilege of self-government of which they have been so long deprived. They themselves, as well as their mode of operation, are so well described in the passage from a recent Parliamentary Report already cited, that I cannot refrain from reproducing it on this occasion, believing, as I do, that it should be read day by day, night by night, month by month, and year by year, until all our people, male and female, young and old, had become thoroughly penetrated with the conviction, that the British proceedings of the past four years had been in perfect harmony with all those of the previous half century, and that if they would not be made mere "hewers of wood and drawers of water" for British capitalists, they must learn to combine among themselves for the adoption of measures of resistance. It is as follows:—

"The laboring classes generally, in the manufacturing districts of this country, and especially in the iron and coal districts, are very little aware of the extent to which they are often indebted for their being employed at all to the immense *losses* which their employers voluntarily incur in bad times in order *to destroy foreign competition, and to gain and keep possession of foreign markets.* Authentic instances are well known of employers having in such times carried on their works at a loss amounting in the aggregate to three or four hundred thousand pounds in the course of three or four years. If the efforts of those who encourage the combinations to restrict the amount of labor and to produce strikes were to be successful for any length of time, the great accumulations of capital could no longer be made *which enable a few of the most wealthy capitalists to overwhelm all foreign competition in times of great depression,* and thus to clear the way for the *whole trade* to step in when prices revive, and to carry on a great business before *foreign* capital can again accumulate to such an extent as to be able to establish a competition in prices with any chance of success. *The large capitals of this country are the great instruments of warfare against the competing capital of foreign countries,* and are *the most essential* instruments now remaining by which our manufacturing supremacy can be maintained; the other elements—cheap labor, abundance of raw material, means of communication, and skilled labor—being rapidly in process of being equalized."

Two centuries since, England sent her wool and her corn to the people of the countries on the Rhine, and took her pay for them in cloth and iron. To her it was a most unprofitable trade. To the Germans it was a most profitable one; so profitable that all Germany wondered at the stolidity of a people who could tolerate its continuance. "The stupid Englishman," as then was said, "sells the skin of a rabbit for a sixpence, and buys back the tail for a shilling." That, my dear sir, is precisely what we have so long been doing—selling cotton at three pence a pound, and buying it back at a shilling an ounce; and giving a bushel of corn for half a dozen pence, the pence themselves to be paid in the form of ounces of corn combined with pennyweights of the three-penny cotton. That sort of taxation it is that "the great capitalists" of England —the men to whom we are indebted for the prolongation of the war, for the expenditure of hundreds of millions of treasure, and the destruction of hundreds of thousands of lives—are determined shall be maintained in all the future.

What are the measures by the aid of which it is that they propose to compel us to its maintenance? To obtain an answer to this question, it is needed that we study a little of the history of the past. British free trade had, in 1842, so far impoverished our people that they were wholly unable to contribute to the support of Government, as a consequence of which many of the States had been driven to repudiation, and the National Treasury had become utterly bankrupt. That state of things it was which gave us, in the passage of the Protective Tariff act of 1842, a new Declaration of Independence. Under it, in less than half a dozen years, there was produced a change such as, to that date, had had no parallel in the history of the world. In that brief period the consumption of coal, iron, and lead was trebled, while that of wool and cotton was doubled. Furnaces and mills were built, labor was everywhere in demand, immigration grew with great rapidity, the public revenue became larger than was needed for meeting all the wants of Government, repudiation passed away, and prosperity once more reigned throughout the land. That, however, not suiting the "great capitalists" above referred to, proprietors of British furnaces and British mills, large sums were raised in 1846, to be so used here as to bring about a change. That they *were* so used in the Senate of the United States, there is no reason for the smallest doubt. By their aid the free-trade tariff of 1846 was made the law of the land, and from the date of its enactment mills and furnaces ceased to be built until California came with its golden treasures to stimulate our people temporarily into action. That tariff lasted eleven years, its existence having been terminated by the still more free-trade tariff of 1857, whose passage proved to be the signal for the crisis of that year which swept away, by thousands, the makers of paper, of cloth, of iron, and of a great variety of commodities for which we became thereafter dependent upon the "great capitalists" of Britain.

In carrying on this British "warfare" against "the competing industry of other countries," the means used are very various, the object to be accomplished being, however, always that of carrying into full effect Lord Brougham's great idea of "destroying," at whatsoever loss, "foreign manufactures in the cradle." The commencement of any new branch of industry has proved to be, and that, I believe, invariably, the signal for an inundation of our markets by goods to be sold at any price until the danger of American competition should have been dispelled. A single case of this, the evidence of which is now before me, may here be mentioned. Ten years since, the price of rough plate glass being then $2 25 per foot, several factories were started, and with the fairest prospects of the most complete success. Forthwith vast quantities were sent here, and the price was reduced to 75 cents. As a necessary consequence our factories ceased to work, their owners were ruined, the "great capitalists," owners of millions, kept "possession of the foreign market," and prices returned again to the point at which it suited the millionaires to hold them. Cases of a similar kind might readily be produced in reference to numerous branches of manufacture.

The grand secret, however, that one which can at will be made available in reference to every branch, is that which manifests itself in the production of AGITATION. These men know well that capitalists are timid, and that past American experience is such as to warrant the extremest caution. When, then, at a commission of five per cent., they employed Messrs. Ashmun, Vinton & Co., during a period of several years, to agitate for the abolition of all duty on railroad iron, they knew that their objects would be fully attained even without the aid of legislation. They knew full well that while that agitation should be continued no man would be so insane as to risk his fortune in a furnace or a rolling-mill. When, now, they use the publishers of books and newspapers for the production of agitation in regard to paper, they have in view that they thereby not only stop the building of paper-mills, but also excite in the minds of our people the strongest doubts in reference to the maintenance of protection in regard to cottons, woollens, and every other department of manufactures. As the battle-cry of Danton was found in the words, *de l'audace, de l'audace, et toujours de l'audace,* so is theirs found in those of agitation, agitation, and always and evermore agitation, for the accomplishment of the great purpose of crushing out all foreign competition for the purchase of the fruits of the earth, and thus compelling all the farmers and planters of the earth to sell their products in Great Britain, and there to make their purchases. To that unceasing agitation it is that we stand indebted for the waste of life and treasure that has been caused by the present great rebellion. To that it is that we are indebted for the fact, that we have been so long and so steadily engaged in selling to our British friends, those *friends* who have so consistently aided in the maintenance of the rebellion, rabbit *skins* for six pence apiece, and taking our pay in rabbit *tails* at a shilling.

If we are ever to do otherwise; if we are to pay the interest of our debt; if we are at any future time to provide for payment of the debt itself; if we are ever again to witness a resumption of specie payments; if we are to have any permanent maintenance of the Union; if we are ever to attain that position among the nations of the world to which our vast natural resources and the extraordinary development of mind among our people so well entitle us; if we are to do our duty to ourselves, to the world at large, and to the Great Being from whom we hold a power for the advancement of the whole human race that is great almost beyond conception; we must put a stop to this agitation. We must do that which will inspire in the minds of timid capitalists, both home and foreign, that confidence which will lead them to apply their means to the development of the wonderful wealth of fuel and of ores of every kind which now lies hidden beneath the soil of almost every State of this great Union. The more that this shall be done, the greater will be the demand for labor; the stronger will be the tendency towards emigration from the shores of Europe; the greater will be the demand for the cotton of the South and the cotton goods of the East, for the fish of the Atlantic coast and the pork of the Mississippi valley; the more rapid will be the growth of that internal commerce so much required for binding together the different portions of the Union; and the more perfect will be the power of our people to furnish the contributions required for the maintenance of the Government to which they will then be indebted for the blessings that have here been named.

The amount required for the support of city, county, State, and Federal governments, and payment of interest on their various debts, cannot be estimated at less than $500,000,000. Of this perhaps $70,000,000 may be obtained at the Custom House. That amount can scarcely be very much exceeded, as it requires an import of little less than $200,000,000

To this add—

For payment of interest on our foreign debt, and dividends on stocks held abroad— . . .	30,000,000
For expenses of absentees, temporary or permanent—	40,000,000
And we obtain a total of	$270,000,000

This is more than we shall be able to pay until cotton, rice, tobacco, and naval stores shall once again take their places in our list of exports. Until now, the earnings of our ships aided in paying for foreign merchandise, but now the balance is against us, and to such an extent as must make a considerable addition to the above amount.

To the Internal Revenue, therefore, must we look for little, if any, less than $450,000,000. To the enforcement of protection we must look for its enlargement, and thus it is that now, more than ever, we are to look to the tariff as the means of raising revenue. The more mills we build, the more mines we sink, the more water-powers we improve, the larger will be the value of land, and the larger will be the revenues of counties and of States. The greater the variety and extent of our manufactures the more numerous will be the exchanges, the greater will be the value of shops and warehouses, and the larger will be the revenues of towns and cities. The greater the quantity of commodities produced the larger will be the contributions of manufacturers towards the Federal revenue. The greater the demand for labor the higher will be wages, and the greater the consumption of tea and coffee, rice and sugar, to the great advantage of that revenue. The larger the reward of labor the greater will be the immigration of laborers, to the great advantage of the owners of the land, and of the men by whom it is tilled. The nearer the market to the farmer the richer will he grow, and the greater will be his power to make, without inconvenience to himself, contributions for the support of the governments of the State and of the Union.

It is the reverse of all this, however, that is desired by the "wealthy capitalists" of Europe. *They* wish to separate the producer and the consumer, and thus to increase to the utmost the tax of transportation. *They* desire that mills and furnaces shall not be built. *They* would have our vast mineral wealth remain undeveloped. *They* would compel us to carry rags and corn to England, to be returned in the form of paper. *They* would have the price of labor kept down to the "famine price," and thus destroy the existing inducements to immigration. *They* would, if they could, drive the government into bankruptcy, and thus forever destroy all hope for any permanent maintenance of the Union.

To that end, they would give us just such agitation as is needed for alarming the great and little capitalists, and preventing the extension of manufactures of any and every kind. The instruments of whose services they avail themselves are—

I. Their own agents, the men in whose hands has now centred nearly the whole business of importation, and who generally succeed in passing their goods through the Custom House at far lower rates of duty than would be paid by our own citizens:

II. Consumers who allow themselves to be dazzled by the idea of obtaining, *for the moment*, goods at low prices, and do not see that low prices abroad are a consequence of that American competition for the sale of similar commodities, in the destruction of which they allow themselves to be engaged:

III. Politicians covetous of the spoils of office, and ready, Samson-like, to pull down the pillars of the temple, if by so doing they can secure the attainment of their ends.

In the hands of men like these—honest men who suffer themselves to be deceived, and dishonest men who desire to deceive others—it is, that "the wealthy capitalists" of England place "the great instruments of warfare against the competing capital of other countries," to be used in the West and the East, in the South and the North, for the maintenance of that agitation which they see to be so much needed. So long as it is kept without the walls of Congress, it does but little harm. When, however, it reaches that body, and when it is thus made necessary for the makers of paper and cloth, iron and steel, to dance attendance, year after year, upon Congressional committees—seeing the sword always suspended over their heads by a single hair, and witnessing always how slight is the perception of many of their members of the importance of the questions to be decided, how trivial the arguments that are brought to bear upon their decisions—it becomes a great national grievance, demanding a remedy that shall likewise be national, and that shall interest the whole of the right-minded and honest people of the country in its application.

In no other country can such difficulties exist. Throughout Europe, and especially in England, the arrangement of revenue laws is the business of specially constituted bodies, with which the legislature readily concurs. With us it is wholly different, each particular portion of a bill having to be examined by men under the influence of local ideas of interest, themselves the result of foreign agitation, and conclusions being arrived at on one day of the discussion that are in direct hostility with those which had been adopted on the preceding one. As a consequence of this, the Executive is frequently compelled to affix his signature to bills of the highest importance, much of which he regards as wholly at war with the national interests. For this no Administration can provide a remedy, and this foreign agitation, with all its tendency towards destruction of confidence in the future, must be continued until the people themselves shall furnish one. From what portion of the people, however, can it come? The poor women now employed in paper-mills, and likely to see themselves sent abroad to seek "other employment" in cities in which the remedy for their distresses is, according to the *Post*, to be found in the reduction of wages to "the famine point," can do nothing towards it. The workmen employed about mills and furnaces that are likely to be closed are equally powerless. The farmers, seeing themselves about to be deprived of the market hitherto furnished by the mill or furnace, are helpless for resistance; while "the wealthy English capitalist," as we have seen, is all-powerful for assault. Whence, then, can resistance come? To what quarter may we look for quieting this unceasing agitation, and for restoring confidence? *To the men through whom the war upon our people is made.* They, and they alone, have power that, if properly directed, will enable the Government to put down agitation, and to establish and maintain such a revenue system as is now so much required.

The daily production of paper is equal to the consumption, and nothing more. The withdrawal of the producers from the market would have the effect of teaching consumers to respect their neighbors' rights. Would such withdrawal be justified? Not only so, but it would be difficult, in my opinion, to justify the former if they failed to address the latter in something like the following terms:—

"*Gentlemen:* Nearly four years have now elapsed since the abdication of Southern Senators and Representatives gave once more to the people of the North the power to assert their rights. Among the earliest measures consequent upon that abdication was a reduction into law of the great idea of the approximation of consumer and producer, so enthusiastically adopted by the Convention which made the Chicago Platform. On that occasion the paper producer was restored to the position he had occupied under the British free-trade tariff of 1846, and nothing more. Shortly after, the closing of Southern ports so far cut off the supply of paper material as to make it doubtful if the needed supply of paper itself could at all be furnished. Since then, our best efforts have been given to the utilizing of other materials, and much, if not even all, of our profits has gone in that direction. So untiring have been our exertions, and so successful have they been, that now, notwithstanding a rise of wages that is wholly without a parallel—notwithstanding a duplication, even where not a triplication, of the cost of every article we use—and notwithstanding the imposition of taxes, direct and indirect, but little short of the duty on the foreign product—we are still enabled to supply you at such prices as wholly forbid the importation of paper from abroad.

"While doing this, we have given support to 50,000 people who might otherwise have been unemployed. We have paid such wages as have enabled them to contribute largely to the support of Government. We have made a market for many millions of dollars' worth of rags, coal, iron, and other commodities, the producers of which have also made large contributions in the same direction. By furnishing a market for labor, we have contributed our full share towards making the country attractive to the millions of Europeans who desire a change of homes; and have in this manner aided in bringing many hundreds of thousands of foreigners to consume the produce of our fields, while engaged in opening mines, building houses, or clearing and making farms for their children and themselves to cultivate.

"Feeling that we have done our duty, both to you and the Government, we regret now to have to say, that the treatment we have received at your hands has scarcely been worthy of your general reputation as men of business, and as Americans. Prompted by 'the wealthy capitalists' of Europe, you have been engaged in an agitation for the destruction of a manufacture that gives large support to the Government, and have thus caused heavy loss to us, while involving in utter ruin some of the largest and most respectable of the producers of the commodity you so much need. You have thus made of yourselves allies of the men who have furnished the means, the money, and the ships that have driven American commerce from the ócean. Like them, you are making war on the public revenue of the country, and should it prove that agitation had in our case been followed by success, further agitation in reference to other branches of industry must be looked for, each in succession resulting in greater loss of revenue, until at length the Government must become bankrupt, and the Union must present to the world a scene of utter chaos, farmers, manufacturers, and traders becoming involved in one common ruin.

"Your power to make this war on the general industry of the country is wholly derived from us. Without our aid it cannot longer be prosecuted. Such being the case, we should deem ourselves guilty of positive crime were we to grant you further aid. So believing, we desire now to notify you, that at the close of a month from this date our mills will stop, and you will then be entirely at liberty to obtain, discharged of any duty, and at a cost to the public revenue of many millions annually, the cheap paper you so much desire.

"Should you think it desirable to engage in the manufacture of an article that is to pay ten or twelve per cent. to the Government if made at home, while coming from abroad free of all such charge, we shall be ready to sell to you our mills, and think you can be assured that they may be purchased at what can be shown to have been their actual cost. Should you fail to accept this proposition you will probably find yourselves, and that at an early day, enabled to judge of the extent to which American competition for the supply of paper has tended to reduce its price generally, and thus to further the cause of civilization throughout the world.

Yours respectfully,

A. B.
C. D.
E. F."

The view above presented is, as I fully believe, a perfectly accurate one, and I cannot but hope that the men who are now being persecuted may manifest the possession of both the patriotism and the resolution required for adopting the course of operation that there is indicated. If the country is to prosper—if the Government is to be sustained—if the Union is to be maintained—it is by means of a policy tending to the approximation of the producer and the consumer, and to the relief of the farmer from the oppressive tax of transportation, and *by that alone*, that those great and essential ends are to be attained.

The real payers of English taxes are the people of the countries that supply the raw materials of manufactures, and buy them back again in a finished form—those who sell the rabbit skin for a sixpence and then repurchase the tail for a shilling. The consequences of this are seen in the fact, that all such countries, poor, weak and despised, are compelled to submit to the dictation of the very people whom they are thus compelled to support. Protection against this tyranny we have at length obtained, and the result is seen in the fact, that our people are now enabled to contribute to the support of Government, and to do so with ease, tens of millions, when before they could with difficulty contribute the millions that were required. This, however, does not suit "the wealthy capitalists" of Britain, and therefore do we find them tempting the consumers of paper and of iron to the work of opening holes in the tariff, well knowing that one which in the outset was large enough to pass only the body of a rat will very speedily become sufficiently large to pass that of an elephant. This must be resisted, and if the paper-makers shall now employ to its full extent the power that is in their hands, they will thereby earn for themselves the thanks of every patriot in the nation; and of all who with me believe that there is *a way to outdo England without fighting her*—a peaceful, pleasant road towards that thorough independence which shall enable us to respect ourselves while commanding the respect of the other nations of the world.

In another letter I propose to ask your attention to some facts concerning the iron manufacture, and meantime remain, my dear sir, with great regard,

Yours respectfully,

HENRY C. CAREY.

Hon. SCHUYLER COLFAX.

PHILADELPHIA, Jan. 2, 1865.

NOTE.—Just as this letter is going through the press I find in the *New York Herald* an article on the subject, from which the following is an extract:—

"There is a movement on foot to induce Congress to repeal the duty on paper. This movement originates out West, and with the editors of republican papers. Some time ago a number of these editors—principally of Chicago and St. Louis papers—met and made their arrangements in the usual way to influence Congress on this subject. They adopted resolutions, appointed committees, delegates, and so on. Their resolutions denounced the duty as onerous to publishers and not beneficial to the Treasury; and their committees and delegates were sent around to influence the press at large, to buttonhole Congressmen and other influential persons, and in all ways to make as much outside pressure as possible. We have been visited on the subject, and were at first glance disposed to aid in the movement, but on a little reflection we are opposed to the whole thing. We are in favor of the duty, and if Congress is disposed to increase it to one hundred or even five hundred per cent. it will be quite agreeable to us.

"In our opinion the Western editors look at this subject through a pinhole, and, consequently, only see a very small part of it. They never consider the subject in any light save that of their own particular interest, and, consequently, they do not understand it at all. They see that the price of paper is high, and they put down their heads and rush at the duty, which they suppose to be the cause; but they rush in the wrong direction. The high price of paper is not in consequence of the duty, and an import duty cannot have any but the most temporary influence on that price. Import duties cannot have any permanent effect on articles that can be produced here of a satisfactory quality. If an article can be made here as well as in foreign countries heavy import duties will only affect the place where it is made. Import duties on such articles merely stimulate domestic manufacture. But, says the man who looks through the pinhole, import duties also protect domestic manufacture, and the high duty that makes the imported article dearer also makes the domestic article bring a higher price. This is not true. Import duties give the market to the domestic product, and the price of the domestic product is regulated, not by that fact, but by demand and competition. If the price of paper is very high, and the demand is great, paper manufactories will spring abundantly into existence wherever capital seeks investment, and prices will find their natural level."

THE IRON QUESTION.

LETTER FIFTH.

DEAR SIR:—

OF all the metals there is none that, in its character of an instrument to be used for facilitating exchanges, does so much as is done by gold in promoting that combination of effort which is the essential characteristic of civilization. It is in that capacity only, however, that it performs such service. Coming to the hands of men ready for use, it makes little demand for combination in its preparation, the golden particles found in the miner's pan being almost as fully fitted for man's service as are the large pieces sent abroad from the mints of this city or of London.

Widely different is it with regard to that greatest of all metals by help of which we cultivate our fields, mine our coal, build our houses, and plate our ships. Coming to us in combination with an almost infinite variety of other materials, it requires all the aid that science can afford to make it fully available for human purposes. Century follows century, each in succession casting new light on its various properties, and with each of them is produced a power for greater combinations of effort, and a necessity for their existence. Thus promoting association it is the great civilizer, and therefore is it that in the extent and growth of its use we find the truest standard by which to test the existence and the growth of civilization. That admitted, and it cannot be denied, we may now proceed to inquire what has been the extent of its use among ourselves, and how far its several stages of growth and decline have been attended, on the one hand by peace and harmony at home, accompanied by growing steadiness of the societary movement; and, on the other, by those frightful crises by which that movement has so often been arrested, and which can be regarded only as the evidences of growing barbarism.

Forty years since, our annual product of this greatest of all metals did not exceed 50,000 tons. Under the semi-protective tariff of 1824 there was a steady increase, but it was not until after the establishment of the thoroughly protective tariff of 1828 that the manufacture attained any large development. By 1832 the product had reached 210,000 tons, and there was then every reason to believe that in a brief period the whole demand would be supplied at home. Prosperity then reigned throughout the land. Public and private revenues were large, and the national debt was in course of rapid annihilation. That, however, not being the state of things desired by "the wealthy capitalists" of England, railroad managers were set to work in and out of Congress, and railroad bars were made wholly free, while the duties on other commodities were left in a great degree unchanged. Shortly after this, however, agitation succeeded in producing a total change of system, the tariff of 1833 having provided for a gradual diminution of all duties, those on iron included, until, in 1842, they should stand at a dead level of 20 per cent. Thenceforward the building of furnaces and mills almost wholly ceased, the "wealthy English capitalists" having thus succeeded in regaining the desired control of the great American market for cloth and iron that had been so nearly lost to them. As a consequence of their triumph there ensued a succession of crises of barbaric tendency, the whole terminating, in 1842, in a scene of ruin such as had never before been known, bankruptcy among the people being almost universal, the banks throughout a large portion of the country being in a state of suspension, States being in a condition of repudiation, and the national treasury being wholly unable to meet its small engagements. Only seven years before, under protection, it had paid off, to the last dollar, the debt of the Revolution.

In 1832, as has been shown, the domestic production of iron having risen to 210,000 tons, civilization was rapidly advancing, with growing power among the people to contribute to the support of Government. Ten years later, with a population one-third greater, the total production of iron being but 230,000 tons, we find a growing barbarism, attended with corresponding decline in the power of the people to pay for maintenance of the trivial fleets and armies that then were needed for self-defence. Such was the result of the employment by British capitalists of that "great instrument of warfare against the competing capital of other countries," by means of which they have thus far succeeded in rendering the Declaration of Independence, issued in 1776, a mere form of words, and so destined to remain until our people shall fully learn that combination for our subjugation needs to be met by *combination for self-defence.*

Universal distress producing a universal demand for remedy, it was furnished by the establishment of that highly protective tariff of 1842, under the influence of which, in less than half a dozen years, the production of iron was carried up to 800,000 tons, and the total consumption of foreign and domestic to 900,000. Six years previously, under British free trade, it had been only 300,000. Here was evidence of advancing civilization, and it was accompanied by that higher evidence which was furnished by the facts that individuals, banks, and States resumed payment of their debts, while the treasury was enabled not only to meet the usual demands upon it, but also to provide, and that without the slightest difficulty, for the expenses of the war with Mexico. Throughout this period there was no excitement, nor was there any crisis. All was peace and harmony, and everywhere in the land there was evidence of rapidly advancing civilization.

The proverb says most truly that "you may bray a fool in a mortar, yet will his foolishness not depart from him." Never, however, has its truth been more fully proved than in these United States. Their people had been "brayed" in the British free trade "mortar" in the terrible period from 1815 to 1825. They had been restored to perfect health in the protectionist period from 1825 to 1835. They had again been "brayed," and to an extent that till then had not been paralleled, in the years from 1835 to 1842. Protection had again restored them in the brief period from 1842 to 1846; yet did they remain so "foolish" as to prove themselves once again open to the blandishments of their excellent *friends* beyond the ocean, "the wealthy capitalists" of Britain, who had been enriched by means of buying their rabbit *skins* at sixpence each and then reselling to them the *tails* at a shilling, and who now found themselves in danger of wholly losing the "foreign markets" they had so long labored to secure. As usual, agitation was recommenced. British agents, with stocks of cheap British goods, were sent to Washington, and the halls of the Capitol were granted to them for the exhibition of their wares. Large sums were raised in England, and politicians here were subsidized. Estimates were furnished to the Senate, in which it was shown that the taxation imposed by the tariff was so oppressive that a ton of nails which could be bought for $90, really cost the purchaser $105 *more* than it would have done under a free trade system; and that a pound of Missouri lead, that could then be bought in New Orleans for $2\frac{3}{4}$ cents, actually cost the consumer three cents *more* than he would have had to pay had he been permitted to get his lead free of duty from Spain or England. Such were the "instruments of warfare" used on that occasion for beating down the system under which the country had so rapidly recovered from the effects of the free trade tariff of 1833. Such were the frauds by means of which the tariff of 1846 was forced upon a country that had already, in the short period of thirty years, twice been "brayed" in the free trade "mortar," and twice had found the effects thereof in an almost entire stoppage of the societary circulation, and an almost absolute bankruptcy of the farmers, traders, bankers, and manufacturers of the country.

Nominally, that tariff came into operation at the end of 1846. Really, it became operative in the summer of 1848, the Irish famine of 1847 having produced a state of things, both abroad and at home, that much delayed its destructive action. From that moment furnaces and rolling mills went gradually out of action until, in 1850, the quantity of iron produced had fallen to less than 500,000 tons. Was the deficiency made up by importation? It was not, the import of that year having exceeded that of 1846 by only 270,000. The whole consumption was, therefore, little more than previously had been the domestic product alone. Nevertheless, our population had then increased but little less than ten per cent. We see thus, that while consumption advances under protection at a rate five times more rapid than that of population, it declines whenever the "wealthy capitalists" obtain the control of the "foreign markets" to which they look with such great anxiety, and for which they are always ready to use that great "instrument of warfare" that we, in our marvellous folly, have placed in their hands, by means of selling *skins* for sixpence and taking our pay in *tails* at a shilling.

The duty under the tariff of 1842 being specific, it underwent no change when prices fell in England. To its full amount, therefore, it constituted an obstacle to importation that it was for the British iron master to remove, paying the cost of removal out of his own pocket and into the Treasury of the Union. As a consequence of this the import of rails in the fiscal year 1846–7, when the country was so highly prosperous, was but one-half as great as the average of the two years preceding the passage of the act of 1842; whereas, the domestic production had risen to 41,000 tons, or little less than double the number imported in those thoroughly free trade years. The total consumption had more than doubled in the short period which had then elapsed, and had thus given evidence that thorough protection and civilization were marching hand in hand together.

The tariff of 1846, with its *ad valorem* duties, came into operation on the first of December of that year, the rate payable by iron being 30 per cent. Fraudulent invoices reduced it, probably, to little more than 20 per cent. American competition had greatly lowered the real British prices, as a consequence of which the amount paid into the treasury by foreign iron and the freight from England combined, during a period of several years, were less than the mere cost of transportation from the furnaces of Pennsylvania to the city of Boston. The "wealthy English capitalists" now profited, and to the fullest extent, of the opportunity thus afforded them "to destroy foreign competition and to gain and keep possession of foreign markets." In 1849 and 1850 the quantity of foreign rails forced on the American market amounted to more than 200,000 tons, while the domestic production of those years averaged but 16,500, although there then existed American mills capable of producing nearly 70,000, and those in a country in which eight years before not a single rail had yet been made.

The furnace master found his market destroyed by the closing of the rolling mill, and the owner of the latter found himself being ruined by the liberal use that then was being made of those "great instruments of warfare," by means of which the "wealthy capitalists" of England had so long been accustomed to annihilate "the competing capital of other countries." In their distress they called on Congress for help, but their cries were totally unheeded. British iron, at the then freights, and almost free of duty, could be delivered here, as then was shown, at $40 per ton; and railroad makers preferred to pay that price for the miserable products of British furnaces, to giving a sliding scale that would secure to the American producer, for sound and excellent iron, the small price of $50, which was *all that then was asked.* Closing their eyes to the fact that it was to American competition for the sale of iron they had been indebted for the low prices of the British markets, they permitted that competition to be almost annihilated, and the competitors to be ruined. The fall of the domestic production from 800,000 tons to less than half a million, produced a necessity for dispensing with its use, or going abroad to purchase all the difference. Competition for purchase in the British market grew as this necessity increased, and therewith came the precise state of things so well described in the Report to which I have so frequently referred—the whole British iron trade having been "enabled to step in when prices revived, and to carry on a great business" before their American competitors could "establish a competition in prices with any chances of success." With the discovery of California gold there arose a great demand for railroad iron, and that demand was, for the first few years, supplied almost entirely from British rolling mills, the railroad makers paying $80 per ton, if not even more, when but a little before they had refused to the domestic producer a sliding scale that would have secured him in the receipt of $50. At enormous prices Britain supplied us, in the four years 1851–54, with no less than a million tons of railroad bars. The additional price paid in those years by American road-makers, as penalty for permitting American competition to be crushed out, could not have been less than $30,000,000, all of which went into British pockets, and thus helped to prepare the way for that new evidence of growing barbarism which was furnished by the terrific crisis of 1857.

In that crisis very many of our iron producers were totally ruined, and the ruin extended itself to all departments of industry connected with this branch of manufacture. The demand for coal diminished, and labor ceased to be required; as a necessary consequence of which immigration rapidly declined, while emigration to Australia, combined with return of the many disappointed, withdrew from us probably one-fourth of all who then were led to seek our shores.

At the breaking out of the rebellion we had been for a whole decade in the ownership of mines that had yielded gold to the extent of more than $500,000,000, and yet we had not been able even to pay our way with Europe. Our foreign debts were probably equal to that sum in their amount. Our credit was so very low that there existed little disposition to purchase further supplies of bonds. As a consequence of this, the importation of railroad iron in the three years 1858–60 averaged but 88,000 tons, and the total consumption of iron, foreign and domestic, but little exceeded that of the closing year of that prosperous protective period which terminated in 1847–8. There is good reason for believing that it did not exceed a million of tons, and yet in the period which had since elapsed our population must have increased more than 40 per cent. Taking then the consumption of iron as the test of civilization, we are presented with the following facts:—

In the six years which followed the passage of the protective act of 1842 the consumption of iron trebled, while the population increased but 20 per cent.

At the end of twelve years from the re-establishment of British free trade, there was but a slight increase, although the numbers of our people had grown 40 per cent.

Bad as was all this, it was but the preparation for those further acts of barbarism which distinguished the close of 1860, and resulted in a civil war that has cost the country hundreds of thousands of lives, and thousands of millions of dollars. Seeking now to find the real cause of that war, and of the destruction of life and property of which it has been the cause, I would ask of you, my dear sir, to read again the Parliamentary Report of the British policy, and then to study carefully the following exhibit of the natural advantages of an important portion of the country that now presents such a scene of devastation.

The great backbone of the Union is found in the ridge of mountains which commences in Alabama but little distant from the Gulf of Mexico, and extends northward, wholly separating the people who inhabit the low lands of the Atlantic slope from those who occupy such lands in the Mississippi valley, and itself constituting a great free soil wedge, with its attendant free atmosphere, created by nature herself in the very heart of slavery, and requiring but a slight increase of size and strength to have enabled its people to control the southern policy, and thus to have brought the entire South into perfect harmony with the North and West, and with the world at large. That you may fully satisfy yourself on this head, I will now ask you to take the map and pass your eye down the Alleghany ridge, flanked as it is by the Cumberland range on the west, and by that of the Blue Mountain on the east, giving, in the very heart of the South itself, a country larger than all Great Britain, in which the finest of climates is found in connection with land abounding in coal, salt, limestone, iron ore, gold, and almost every other material required for the development of a varied industry, and for securing the attainment of the highest degree of agricultural wealth; and then to reflect that it is a region which must necessarily be occupied by men who with their own hands till their own lands, and one in which slavery can never by any possibility have more than a slight and transitory existence. That done, I will ask of you here to reflect what would be now the condition of the Union had its policy for the last twenty years been such as would have tended towards *filling this great free soil wedge with free white northern men*—miners, smelters, founders, machinists—workmen of all descriptions—who should have been making a market for every product of the farm, with constant increase in the value of land and labor, and as constantly growing tendency towards increase of freedom for all men, whether black or white? Would not, under such circumstances, power have made its way to the hills, and would not iron, coal, limestone, and copper have been enabled to dictate law to the cotton kings—to the men who occupied on the river bottoms, and lived at ease at the cost of those of their fellow-men whom they bought and sold in the open market? Could we, by any possibility, have witnessed the present extraordinary state of things, had the policy of the country in reference to domestic and foreign commerce not been directed by the "wealthy capitalists" who are now so busily engaged in making rat-holes through the existing tariff, very moderately protective as it is? Most assuredly we should not. *To* them it is that we are indebted for our present troubles and our debt, and *of* them it is we should exact the payment of it. That, however, we shall never do if we shall continue to sell rabbit *skins* for sixpence and take our pay in rabbit *tails* for a shilling.

Why have we so long continued so to do? Because, although Independence was declared in 1776, we have never pursued the policy required for making the declaration any more than a mere word of small significance. With slight exception we have been governed by the great capitalists of Britain, and have pursued the precise system that was advocated in England before the Revolution as the one required for retaining the Colonies in a state of vassalage, and thus compelling them to so make the unprofitable exchanges to which I have referred. What was that system is fully shown in an English work of much ability, published in London at the time when Franklin was urging upon his countrymen the diversification of their pursuits, as the only road towards real independence, and from which the following is an extract:—

"The population, from being spread round a great extent of frontier, would increase without giving the least cause of jealousy to Britain; land would not only be plentiful, but plentiful where our people wanted it, whereas, at present, the population of our colonies, especially the central ones, is confined; they have spread over all the space between the sea and the mountains, the consequence of which is, that land is becoming scarce, that which is good having all been planted. The people, therefore, find themselves too numerous for the agriculture, which is the first step to becoming manufacturers, that step which Britain has so much reason to dread."

Why, my dear sir, should Britain have so much dreaded combination among her colonial subjects? Why should she so sedulously have sought to disperse them over the extensive tracts of land beyond the mountains? Because, the more they scattered the more dependent they could be kept, and the more readily they could be compelled to carry all their rude products to a distant market, there to sell them so cheaply, as we are told by another distinguished British writer, "that not one-fourth of the product redounded to their own profit," as a consequence of which plantation mortgages were most abundant, and the rate of interest charged upon them so very high as generally to eat the mortgagor out of house and home. In a word, the system of that day, as described by those writers, was almost precisely that of the present hour. For its maintenance, dispersion of the population was regarded as indispensable, and that it might be attained, the course of action here described was recommended:—

"Nothing can therefore be more politic than to provide a superabundance of colonies to take off all those people that find a want of land in our old settlements; and it may not be one or two tracts of country that will answer this purpose: provision should be made for the convenience of some, the inclination of others, and every measure taken to inform the people of the colonies that were growing too populous, that land was plentiful in other places, and granted on the easiest terms; and if such inducements were not found sufficient for thinning the country considerably, government should by all means be at the expense of transporting them. Notice should be given that sloops would be always ready at Fort Pitt, or as much higher on the Ohio as is navigable, for carrying all furniture without expense, to whatever settlement they chose, on the Ohio or Mississippi. Such measures, or similar ones, would carry off the surplus of population in the central and southern colonies, which have been and will every day be more and more the foundation of manufactures."

Having studied these recommendations in regard to the maintenance of colonial dependence, I will ask you now to study the working of the British free trade system, and satisfy yourself that its advocates, the *agitators* of whom I have spoken, have been mere instruments of our foreign masters—closing our mills, furnaces, and factories, retarding the development of our great mineral treasures, preventing the utilization of our vast water powers, and in this manner scattering our people, in strict accordance with the orders of those British traders against whom our predecessors made the Revolution.

Having now brought up this review of the iron trade to the period of the great rebellion, I propose in another letter to bring it down to the present time, and then to show what are the measures by which we may be enabled to *outdo England without fighting her*, and thus establish a real independence.

Yours, very truly,

HENRY C. CAREY.

Hon. SCHUYLER COLFAX.

PHILADELPHIA, Jan. 6, 1865.

THE IRON QUESTION.

LETTER SIXTH.

Dear Sir:—

The preparation seems to have now been made for boring another hole through the protective system that has recently been so well established. This time it takes the form of a protest, of course in favor of the public revenue, against duties on spool cotton, under which, as we are told, "foreign spinners are now suffering in their attempts to contend against these heavy odds whereby importation is now stopped." Large exhibits are made therein of the quantity of gold that is thus prevented from passing into the treasury, but not a word is said in reference to the important fact, that, under the system which has thus far made us dependent on Britain for that important commodity, we have never yet been able to carry up our consumption even to the amount of six cents per head of our population. Selling cotton at three or four pence per pound we have been required to pay in gold, to the extent of millions of dollars per annum, for pennyweights of it combined with Russian and Egyptian corn, while the farmer of Iowa, unable to find a market for his grain, has found it expedient to convert it into fuel, and thus prevent its total waste. Here, as everywhere, we have been favoring the policy of slavery and barbarism, limiting our people to the raising of raw produce for the supply of distant masters, by whom they have been required to give the whole skin for a sixpence, receiving their pay in tails at a shilling. The answer to all that is now said in regard to the opening of the new rat-hole which is now proposed, is found in the words of the excellent article from the *Herald*, a part of which was appended to a former letter: "*If the price is very large and the demand is great, manufactories will spring abundantly into existence and prices will find their natural level.*" If the British manufacturers are really suffering in the manner above described, let them transfer themselves and their machinery here; let them bring their people with them to eat the food of Illinois and Iowa in place of that of Egypt; let them do this and the price of their commodity will soon be so far lessened that our consumption will rise to 20 cents per head; the Government will then receive, in the form of internal revenue, an amount far greater than these foreign agitators ever yet have paid at the custom-house; and we shall then have made a further step towards enabling ourselves to retain at home the gold that we ourselves shall so much need when the time shall have arrived for using the precious metals in the place of paper.

Having thus disposed of this new subject of agitation, the further examination of the great Iron Question comes now next in order.

To British free trade it is, as I have shown, that we stand indebted for the present civil war. Had our legislation been of the kind which was needed for giving effect to the Declaration of Independence, that great hill region of the South, one of the richest, if not absolutely the richest in the world, would long since have been filled with furnaces and factories, the laborers in which would have been free men, women, and children, white and black, and the several portions of the Union would have been linked together by hooks of steel that would have set at defiance every effort of the "wealthy capitalists" of England for bringing about a separation. Such, however, and most unhappily, was not our course of operation.

Rebellion, therefore, came, bringing with it an almost entire stoppage of the societary movement, with ruin to a large proportion of those of the men engaged in producing coal and iron who had still continued to exist notwithstanding the heavy losses inflicted upon them in the sad five years which had just then elapsed. More than at any previous period the Government stood then in need of iron in all its shapes, from the needle with which the poor sewing woman makes the shirt, to the great sheet required for plating the enormous ship of war; and yet, such had been the extraordinary policy of the country that, while fuel abounded rolling mills were idle and furnaces were out of blast, and the machinery for the needle and the plate had not as yet been permitted to take its place at any single point over our extensive surface. As a consequence, poor as was then our Government, and unemployed as were then so large a portion of our people, we were compelled to send abroad for millions upon millions of dollars worth of the machinery of war, and there to encounter all the obstacles that could decently be thrown in our way by men who prayed openly for the success of the rebellion, and who, almost at the instant of its first occurrence, had, by royal proclamation, placed the rebel Government on a level with that which their predecessors had, in 1783, so unwillingly recognized. This great adversity had, however, brought with it a remedy that, if now properly applied, will cause our children and our children's children to look back to the period of its occurrence as that in which there had been an act of Providential interference in favor of a community such as had had no precedent in the history of the world, prompting, as it had done, men who for seventy years had wholly controlled the action of the Government, to abdicate their seats and leave the direction of affairs to those who represented the poor and despised "mud-sills" of northern States. So great an act of insanity had never before been perpetrated by any body of intelligent men, and, most fortunately, its perpetration occurred at the moment when the public opinion of the North had been prepared to profit of it.

That preparation had come as a natural consequence of the terrific free trade crisis of 1857. Assembling in 1860, the politicians at Chicago accepted most unwillingly that new plank of the platform by which "protection to the farmer in his efforts for bringing the consumer to his side" was incorporated into the Republican creed; and great was their surprise when they found that public opinion, and especially the opinion of the great Mississippi Valley, had left them far behind. "We might have made it stronger," was the exclamation of one of its chief opponents after he had witnessed the enthusiastic applause with which it had been greeted. As yet, however, it could be nothing more than a declaration of good intentions to be carried into effect at some future time, the senatorial power appearing then likely long to remain in the hands of men who believed in human slavery as the corner-stone of all free government; in British free trade as the means by which slavery was to be perpetuated and extended throughout this continent; and in the "wealthy capitalists" of England, as the firm allies by whose aid their ambitious hopes were to be fully realized. To give practical effect to the new Declaration of Independence, it was necessary that those men should abdicate, and happily for the North, and for the world, abdication was not long delayed. Protection then at once became the law of the land, and under circumstances that should have tended to free forever the country from that agitation by means of which the British trader had so long controlled the societary movement, and had, with so much profit to himself, been enabled to fill the British treasury by means of taxes, direct and indirect, upon nearly all the foreign exchanges that our poverty had permitted us to make. Between skins at sixpence and tails at a shilling—cotton at cents per pound and cotton goods at shillings per ounce—corn at cents per bushel and wool and corn at dollars per pound—there was a large margin for the British trader and his superiors, and out of the taxes thus extorted have, to a large extent, the British nation and its government been supported by the people of these United States. Protection looked to the abolition of this taxation. That it has done much in that direction is proved by the great fact, that it has enabled us to contribute thousands of millions of dollars towards the suppression of the rebellion; that it has in so short a period given us a navy such as had been so long required for setting at naught the declaration that "not a flag but by permission spreads;" and that, notwithstanding all our vast expenditures, the productive power of the loyal States is greater at this moment than was that of the whole Union on the day on which, less than four years since, President Lincoln assumed the reins of government.

The need for iron soon became very great. Great, too, was the disposition of iron men to exert themselves for the supply of the wants the rebellion had now created. The Government had just then pledged itself to stand by them in their contest for the market of the world, at home and abroad, with the men who had so long controlled "that great instrument of warfare" by whose judicious use their predecessors had so generally been ruined. The pledge was accepted, and the results exhibit themselves in the facts:—

I. That the production of pig-iron has already been carried up to more than 1,300,000 tons, and that it has been made certain that large as is the quantity, it can with ease, provided that the labor can be obtained, be trebled in the next seven years:

II. That the rolling-mills of the country have now a capacity of nearly 700,000 tons, and that the only difficulty now standing in the way of the production of that quantity of sheet and bars is the one resulting from the scarcity of labor:

III. That the supply of railroad iron is now fully equal to the demand, and can be increased to any extent that may be required:

IV. That the conversion of iron into steel has been so much extended as to free us entirely from any further dependence on the "wealthy capitalists" of Britain:

V. That works required for the conversion of steel and iron into the various other machinery required for both public and private uses have been so extended as to enable their proprietors to meet the whole demand.

The industrial history of the world exhibits nothing at all comparable with what has here been done in regard to this great branch of manufacture. That it might be done every man who previously had been interested therein has been required to apply to the enlargement and improvement of his machinery not only every dollar that he could make, but, in very many cases, all that he could borrow; and this they have done in the false confidence that consumers of iron had at last so far profited of past experience as to have become convinced that the way to have good and cheap iron was to be found in the direction of stimulating competition for its manufacture; and not in that of annihilating American competition for its *sale*, while promoting competition for its *purchase* from the very men who had always used their power in the direction of promoting agitation for the destruction of "foreign competition," and for enabling themselves to "gain and keep possession of foreign markets."

That it *was* a false confidence you will, my dear sir, see, after you shall have accompanied me in a brief review of the proceedings of iron consumers which it is proposed now to make. When you shall so have done, you will, as I think, agree with me that it would be difficult to find in the history of the world a case in which the proverb given in my last had been more thoroughly applicable than it now is in reference to the iron consumers of these United States. Often as they had been "brayed" in the British free trade "mortar," their "foolishness" had not departed from them.

By the tariff of 1861 the duty on railroad iron was fixed at $12 per ton of 2,240 pounds, being less than one-half of the charge upon it as established by the tariff of 1842—that one under which iron generally was so cheaply furnished that the total consumption of the country was in four years carried up from 300,000 to 900,000 tons. It should have been placed at a higher rate than this, and so it would have been but for the exceedingly absurd and stupid jealousy which prompts so many persons to consider the iron manufacture the special property of Pennsylvania. Iron ore abounds in more than two-thirds of the States of the Union; fuel, too, almost as much abounding as the ore demanding to be smelted; and it is to the great credit of Pennsylvania that her ironmasters have never in a single instance allowed themselves to be influenced by the narrow idea, elsewhere openly expressed in regard to other branches of manufacture, that it was needed to "keep protection down, lest it might stimulate domestic competition." If there are any ironmasters in the country who can live without protection, they are those of that State. They are the men who have paid most dearly for their experience. To them the country is indebted for the fact that this great branch of manufacture, in nearly all its processes, is now ahead of Britain. They, however, know that Tennessee and Alabama, Missouri and Michigan, Virginia, Maryland, and Ohio, need protection; and they desire that they shall have it, quite assured that in the wide extension and general prosperity of the manufacture in which they are so well engaged will be found the key to that universal prosperity which enables men to extend their roads, to increase and improve their machinery, and to do all those things that make demand for iron and thus furnish proof conclusive of advancing civilization. Least in need of it, they stand foremost in the demand for efficient protection, asking it in the interest of the country at large, and not, as is in so many other cases done, exclusively in their own.

Accepting the rate of duty that had been fixed, they went promptly to work, and with the results that have been shown. The time came, however, when it became necessary to establish a system of Internal Revenue, and railroad iron was then subjected to a direct tax of $1 50 per ton, while upon coal and other commodities used in its production heavy duties were imposed. Incomes, too, were required to contribute, the general rate of contribution, by both the manufacturer and the receiver of income, being fixed at *three* per cent.

The war having thus produced a necessity for taxing both the materials of manufacture and its products, it was deemed proper to subject the foreign manufacturer to the payment of a like contribution, and duties generally were raised to the extent of *five* per cent. To this, however, railroad iron was made an exception, the addition having been limited to the precise amount of the direct tax, $1 50 per ton, and no allowance whatever having been made for the taxes on coal, lime, machinery, or incomes. Such, my dear sir, was the paltry spirit in which were met the men who were at that moment, in their efforts to meet the wants of the Government, manifesting a larger liberality than any other body of men that could have been produced in the whole extent of the Union.

The necessity for further revenue becoming obvious, the last session of Congress gave us a new excise law by means of which pig metal was for the first time subjected to a tax, and that to the extent of two dollars per ton, the tax on coal being at the same time largely increased, and that on rails more than doubled, the general effect being that of giving a tax on the rail itself amounting to seven dollars per ton.

To this must now be added taxes on lime and other raw materials—taxes on machinery to a large amount—income taxes—taxes on licenses—taxes on sales—taxes on freights—taxes on leases—taxes on salaries—taxes on charters, notes of hand, and articles of agreement—the whole of which, when added to the $7 already obtained, will give at least $8 50 as the contribution in these several forms to be paid by each ton of railroad bars.—Adding now to this the large increase, consequent upon the existence of the war, of state, county, township, and borough taxes—the contributions for obtaining volunteers and for maintaining their families, it will be found that the amount, under this new law, furnished by each ton of bars, for the maintenance of the contest, cannot be estimated at less than $10.

Having thus shown what was the pressure brought by the Government to bear upon the men who were giving all their time, mind, and means to building up that great manufacture on which now rests the whole of our great societary machine, *and upon whose success or failure is dependent the whole future of this Union,* I propose in my next to show what were the measures at the same time adopted by the Government for enabling them successfully to compete with those "wealthy English capitalists" who were then giving all their time, mind, and means to the work of vilifying our people, destroying our credit, breaking our blockades, destroying our ships, and in every other way aiding a rebellion whose success, as they saw, could have no other result than that of reducing the country to a state of complete dependence.

It is with great regret, my dear sir, that I make so many demands upon your time and attention, but the question now to be settled is one of so great importance that you will, I am sure, excuse me.

When the present war shall have been closed there will be another to be fought, and that one will be with England. By many it is desired that it may be a war of cannon balls; but it is not now with such machinery that she chiefly seeks to fight us. It is in the Halls of Congress she is to be met, and the machinery with which we have successfully to meet her is to be found in the adoption of those measures which shall enable us most speedily to profit of that inexhaustible store of fuel and of ores that nature has placed at our command. So believing, and hoping that all my countrymen may soon be led to the conclusion that there really is a way to *outdo England without fighting her*, I am, with great regard and respect,

Yours, very truly,

HENRY C. CAREY.

Hon. SCHUYLER COLFAX.

PHILADELPHIA, Jan. 9, 1865.

THE IRON QUESTION.

LETTER SEVENTH.

DEAR SIR :—

That the power to prosecute the war in which we are engaged has been derived mainly from the Mining States, must be obvious to all who take the trouble to reflect that for the force by which our mills have been driven and our blockade maintained, and the iron by means of which that force has been applied, the Union has had to look almost entirely to the mountains of Pennsylvania. But for the energy with which the mineral resources of that State have been developed the war could not have been maintained for even a single year. To their further development, and to that of her sister Mining States, the Union has now to stand indebted for its power to collect the revenue by means of which its credit is to be maintained, its wars, present and future, to be carried on, and its debt ultimately discharged. *Failing to secure that development it must itself prove a failure, absolute and complete.*

Seeing this, and it is so clearly obvious that it would appear difficult that any should fail to do so, it might be supposed that coal and iron, as the foundation upon which now rests, and must in all the future rest, our whole societary movement, would, in these trying times, and after the sad experience of the *blessings* of British free trade, have been regarded as *entitled to peculiar care.* That prior to the last Session of Congress they had not been so regarded, and that, on the contrary, of the little that had been given by one hand much had been taken away by the other, has been already shown. That the movement since that time has been in the same unfortunate direction, it is proposed now to show.

The total taxation of a ton of railroad bars, for the maintenance of the war, cannot be taken at less than $10. Before the passage of any tax law the duty had been fixed at $12, that having been the smallest sum to which it had been possible to obtain the assent of the Mining States. Under the first tax law the charges of the Government to the domestic producer may be taken as having been not less than $3, while the additional payment required of the foreign producer was limited to $1 50. Since then the former have been more than trebled, and it would have been but just to carry up the latter to the same extent, thereby compelling the British iron master to pay $20. Instead of that, his contribution was *reduced* to the point at which it had stood on the day on which Fort Sumter fell. Such was the manner in which the decision of the Chicago Convention was carried into effect in regard to a manufacture upon the success or failure of which was wholly dependent the answer to be given to the questions as to whether or not the Government was to be sustained; whether or not the interest on the debt was to be paid; whether or not specie payments should ever be resumed; whether or not the national debt should ever be discharged?

It may, however, be said that the duty of $12 is payable in gold, while the $10 of taxes are payable in paper, and such is certainly the case. *That difference now constitutes the sole protection to this great branch of manufacture.* When, however, is it to cease? Who can tell what time is to elapse before some enterprising financier shall succeed in persuading the Government to the adoption of measures tending to the sudden reduction, at any cost to the people, of gold to par? Such measures are, as we all know, now advocated in some of the most influential Republican journals, and they have, as I have good reason to believe, received the approbation of men of the highest standing connected with the Administration. That they would be suicidal in their tendency cannot be received as furnishing even the slightest evidence that they will not be adopted, seeing that we have now before us evidence that gentlemen connected with railroads have so entirely failed to profit by experience which should have taught them that the cheap British iron of 1864 was but the trap by help of which they were to be made to pay probably twice the price for just such iron, poor as it generally is, in 1866. Time and again have they and their predecessors been brayed in the British "mortar," yet has their "foolishness" not yet departed from them.

The direct contribution of pig and bar iron to the revenue can scarcely this year be taken, as I think, at less than $5,000,000. Add to this the taxes on coal, lime, transportation, incomes, &c. &c. &c., and we shall obtain probably double that amount. This would seem to be a large sum to put at risk, and yet it is as nothing compared with the extent of risk that is to be incurred, the coal and iron trades of the country constituting the foundation upon which this day rests our whole system of internal revenue. Break *them* down, as they will be broken if the system be not promptly changed, and the Government will, before the lapse of even a single year, become so utterly bankrupt that its certificates of indebtedness will have little more value in the public eye than have this day those of the so-called Confederacy of the Southern States.

To those who may entertain any doubts on this subject I would recommend reflection on the following facts:—

I. The consumption of iron is the test of growing civilization, strength, and power.

II. That consumption doubled in the protective period from 1828 to 1834, our numbers meanwhile increasing but 20 per cent.

III. Eight years later, in 1842, with British free trade and an increase of numbers amounting to 30 per cent., the quantity consumed had made scarcely any progress whatsoever.

III. Thence to 1848, under protection, with a growth of population of but 20 per cent., it trebled—having already reached the large amount of 900,000 tons.

IV. Twelve years now follow, spent under the British free trade system, giving us—an increase of population to the extent of nearly 40 per cent.—the great discovery of California gold with corresponding increase in the necessity for internal intercourse—and an increase in the consumption scarcely, if at all, exceeding 12 per cent.

V. In the three years that have now elapsed since the Morrill tariff became fairly operative, the population subject to it has been less by a third than that of 1860, and yet the consumption now exceeds 1,300,000 tons, having increased more than 30 per cent.

In the first and third of these periods every branch of manufacture was prosperous, and the power of the people, at their close, to contribute to the support of Government was thrice greater than it had been at their commencement.

In the second and fourth every branch of manufacture was prostrate, and the power at their close to contribute to the support of Government had been almost entirely annihilated.

In the fifth there has been an activity of commerce that before had not been paralleled, as a consequence of which our people have been enabled to contribute to the support of Government hundreds of millions, and with far more ease than in 1860 they could have furnished tens of millions. Our whole experience proves, then, that power for maintaining the Government grows or declines almost geometrically as the consumption of iron increases or decreases arithmetically.

Having reflected on the facts thus presented, I would now, my dear sir, beg you to answer to yourself if our iron consumers, in the course they have recently adopted, have not furnished proof conclusive that they are of the same race precisely with the Bourbons, of whom it was said on their return to France on the downfall of Napoleon, that they had not profited by their long experience of the troubles of exile to learn anything they had not previously known, or to forget any of the prejudices with which they had started. Both alike had been "brayed in the mortar" of experience, yet had they remained as "foolish" as at first.

Such having been the course pursued in regard to this great fundamental branch of manufacture, let us now look to that presented in reference to another and very subordinate branch that has just now been brought into discussion—that of spool cotton. By the tariff of 1861, the duty thereon was fixed at 24 per cent. By that of 1862 it was raised to 30 per cent. That of 1863 made it 40. Again raised in 1864, we find it to be a combination of specific and ad-valorem duties that compels the foreign producer to pay more than four times as much in gold as is paid by the domestic one in paper. The domestic iron producer, on the contrary, pays nearly as much in paper as the foreign one pays in gold. The domestic paper producer pays more than half as much in paper as the foreign manufacturer pays in gold, the great fundamental industries being thus almost entirely abandoned to the "tender mercies" of "wealthy English capitalists," while the minor ones are placed in a condition to feel themselves entirely secure.

The "absurdity" of all this is most remarkable, the market for thread, cloth, books, and all other commodities being almost wholly dependent upon the prosperity of the great coal, iron, and paper producing interests. Such legislation would find its fittest legislator in the man who should spend his mornings in carefully trimming the branches of his trees while his evenings were as assiduously employed in cutting away their roots.

To what cause is such "absurdity" to be attributed? In great part to the existence of that powerful British combination so well described in the Report to Parliament heretofore given, and in no inconsiderable part to a necessity that was, at the date of the Congressional action above described, supposed to exist for "punishing Pennsylvania." Almost inconceivable as it may seem that such should be the grounds on which was based the decision of one of the greatest of national questions, that it was so based there is not, as I believe, the smallest reason to doubt. Assuming it so to have been, it may not be, my dear sir, improper here to ask your attention to a few facts in relation to the past and present of the great State which then was held to stand so much in need of *punishment.*

As New England furnishes us the type of that portion of our population which has occupied New York, the northern edge of Pennsylvania, northern Ohio, Indiana, and Illinois, Michigan, and other Northwestern States, so do Pennsylvania and New Jersey give us the type of the population of a great belt of territory, 120 miles in breadth, and ten times that in length, now containing more than 10,000,000 of as industrious and active people as can be found elsewhere throughout the world. When, therefore, Pennsylvania speaks, she does so as the representative of the opinion of all those millions, and therefore is it—and not because of her own particular strength—that it has grown into a proverb, that *as Pennsylvania goes, so goes the Union.*

How *has* she gone in those two great crises which, since the peace of 1783, most have "tried men's souls"—those of the institution in 1788 of the present government, and at later ones of the past four years? Let us see.

The Constitution, as adopted by the Convention of 1788, placed the smaller States, as regarded Senatorial representation, on an equal footing with the larger ones, and hence gave great offence to nearly all of these latter. The single exception to this was found in Pennsylvania, which, first of all to consider that great instrument, was first of all, with the single exception of the little State of Delaware, to ratify it. Months elapsed before her example was followed by Massachusetts and Virginia, while something closely resembling compulsion was required before it was accepted by New York.

In that great crisis Pennsylvania, by her remarkable magnanimity, earned the title of the Keystone State, but whether or not it was then that it was given to her, I have no means of knowing. Certain it is, that but for her prompt and decided action the Union, as it since has been, would never have been accomplished.

Coming now to the second great crisis, that in which we are now involved, let us see how she has gone, and how far her action has tended to maintain that Union which had been indebted to her for all its previous existence.

I. Scarcely had the first call of the President been fully met before she applied herself diligently to the creation of a large and fully appointed army, whose acceptance was urged upon the Government. Had it been accepted, the Bull Run battle would probably have had a very different termination. Had it not existed, the war might, and probably would, then have ended in the capture of Washington.

II. In three years and a half she has furnished to the army, exclusive of militia and ninety days volunteers, above 300,000 men, or more than a tithe of her whole population. Had all the loyal States done as much, the whole number supplied by them would have exceeded 2,000,000. Always among the first, even when not actually first in point of time, she has never been behind any in point of numbers.

III. Always ready in the field, she has been equally so at the polls. When New York had abandoned the national cause, and when the whole future of the country had become dependent upon the question whether she would, or would not, place herself side by side with that State and New Jersey and thus cripple the Federal Government, she gave in her adhesion to the great cause, and by a majority that, allowing for the absent troops, was greater than it had been at the first. Had she acted differently on that occasion, the war must have come to an end, and the Union must have ceased to exist. From first to last, therefore, she has proved herself to be *the Keystone State.*

IV. In her Commercial Capital, she has given the most loyal city of the Union; the one that has, in proportion to its means, furnished the largest contributions; that one which alone has fed the tired and hungry soldier, from whatsoever State he has hailed; and that one towards which the cold shoulder of the Government has invariably been turned.

Such having been the course which has so recently subjected her to "punishment," we may now, my dear sir, without impropriety, look for a moment to the machinery by means of which it has been administered. As it was at the time explained to me, it was as follows: Leader in the action was a British agent, representative of those "wealthy English capitalists," who furnish "great instruments of warfare against the competing capital of other countries," by means of which they "gain and keep possession of foreign markets." Iron being abundant and cheap in England, a considerable quantity had been shipped to him, and he was naturally anxious to economize the contribution to be paid thereon to the Federal Government—that one for whose destruction his masters were then so anxiously laboring. As it chanced, some little Western roads stood in pressing need of iron, and money was then so scarce with them that the saving of a few thousand dollars thereon was deemed a matter of much importance. For accomplishing that saving it was needed that they should obtain a change in the tariff law. Forthwith, they and their English friends set themselves to *prove* that the wear and tear of roads was twice as great as it really had been, the producing power of American mills being at the same time *proved* to be less than half of what we know to be its actual amount. Other roads, the managers of which were thus deceived, were led to lend their aid. To these were now to be added all of the men in Congress who desired to see the Government reduced to bankruptcy, and thus was formed a "ring" of size sufficient to "punish Pennsylvania." The deed was done, and thus was at once destroyed all confidence in the permanence of a system that had been received by the world as confirmation by Congress of that remarkable expression of the public will given at the Convention held in Chicago five years since. For its destruction there was given, as I believe, the vote of nearly every man who has on all occasions opposed the Government in its efforts to maintain the national credit, they well knowing, as I doubt not, that in crippling the iron manufacture, and in punishing its chief representative, they were rendering the largest service in their power to the rebellious States.

That this is a correct statement of the means by which that discreditable action was brought about, I entertain no doubt. Admitting for the moment that it is so, does it not present a state of things of which we have reason to feel much ashamed? In what other nation, making any claim to civilization, are miserable foreign emissaries permitted thus to prowl through the halls of legislation? Were such things tolerated in England or in France, should we hold those nations in much respect? Could they respect themselves? Can we claim the existence of anything like self-respect while such profligate and impertinent meddling with our affairs shall continue to be tolerated? As it appears to me, we certainly cannot.

Having shown the past of the great State which has thus, and at the hands of a wretched foreign broker, received the "punishment" she had so well earned, I desire now to ask you to look for a moment at her present, with a view to the determination of the question what should be her action in the future.

Four years since, she and Virginia presented the types of two great sections of the Union, the one north, and the other south, of Mason and Dixon's line, the Ohio and the Missouri. On one side was the freedom which always accompanies the connection of agriculture with manufactures. On the other was the slavery which always accompanies that exclusive devotion of labor to the work of supplying distant markets which Britain and Carolina have always sought to perpetuate. On both sides there existed a belief in the necessity for measures of protection, except in the single, and then dominant, State of Virginia. Since then, however, she has abdicated, and freedom has taken, or is now rapidly taking, the place of slavery throughout the whole of that region of country, the richest in the world in regard to metals of almost every kind. Her abdication has placed the *punished* Pennsylvania now in the lead of all the Mining States, embracing a territory of 600,000 square miles, throughout which coal, iron, lead, copper, gold, and other metals so much abound that labor alone is needed for carrying up, within the next twenty years, their production to an extent far greater than the present consumption of the entire world. To the development of that wealth we have to look if we would sustain the Government and maintain the Union. To it must we look if we would maintain our credit and pay our debts. To it alone can we look if we would sink so deeply the foundations of our great public edifice as to secure for it that stability of action which is needed to give it permanence. Upon this, however, through one of her little deputies, Britain has put her *veto*, thereby *punishing* Pennsylvania for making the attempt.

What now should the latter do? Should she sit still while the foundations of our system are being undermined? Should she tolerate a policy thus forced upon the nation by foreign agents, that *must* end in her own ruin, and that of her sister States? Should she longer tolerate the impertinent interference of British brokers in affairs of such high importance? That she should not, I feel well assured. What then should she do?

She ought to invite a Convention, representing the people of all the Mining States, in population comprising probably three-fifths of the whole Union, and in national resources, three-fourths, with a view to *that combination of effort which is needed for enabling us to free the country from this foreign dictation.* She should proclaim her intention to seek, by all constitutional means, to make of the Declaration of Independence something of more value than would be an equal quantity of mere blank paper. She should say to the people of the whole of those States, that she desired to secure for herself and them that protection which would enable them to unite in supplying the world, both abroad and at home, with iron, confidently relying upon a growth of demand that would keep pace with growth of supply, and thus furnish evidence of increasing strength and advancing civilization. To the people outside of the Mining States she should say, that the more iron made at home the greater would be the demand for cotton and sugar, and for cotton and woollen goods; that among the various portions of the country there was a perfect harmony of interests; that in her efforts at stimulating into activity the great resources of the centre, she was giving her energies towards securing happiness and prosperity to the people of the north, south, east, and west; and, that in thus presenting a mode of *outdoing England without fighting her*, she was doing that which was required for enabling all to enjoy in peace the grand results which must be obtained from the suppression of the great rebellion.

Twice already in great crises has she proved her claim to her title of *Keystone State.* Let her do so once again; let her now do what it is clearly in her power to do, for giving practical effect to the Declaration of Independence; let her show to the world that power, wealth, credit, prosperity, and happiness, may be procured by means of peaceful measures that shall at the same time give us satisfaction for all past injuries received from abroad; and she will thereby earn the thanks of every American, every friend of peace, every lover of his kind, every Christian throughout the world.

Having thus shown what is, as I think, the duty of what is now the leading iron-producing State, I propose, in another letter, to show what it is that I deem to be the duty of the iron producers, and meanwhile remain, with great regard and respect,

Yours, very truly,

HENRY C. CAREY.

Hon. Schuyler Colfax.

Philadelphia, January 11, 1865.

THE IRON QUESTION.

LETTER EIGHTH.

Dear Sir:—

For every ton of railroad bars now made here, the maker is required to contribute for the support of the war and for maintenance of the public credit, at least *ten dollars*. For every ton of British bars imported the manufacturer is required to contribute for the same purposes, the sum of *twelve dollars*. For every ton of the first transported, the producer is required to pay into the treasuries of American railroad companies, and to the owners of American vessels—both large contributors to the Public Revenue—a sum that is, probably, on an average, little less than twice as great as are the freights from abroad of that British iron which comes in British ships, owned by the men who are now using their best efforts in the advocacy, and in the material support, of the rebellion.* *Their* vessels pay nothing in the shape of tonnage duties, nothing for the use of lights that are maintained by us at heavy cost. *Their* owners pay no excise duties on their iron. *They* have their coal free of duty, and at a third of the cost of that used by our ships. *They* are free from the thousand claims upon their means which now compel our people to such high charges as have almost driven from the ocean the Stars and Stripes. Those charges must continue if we would maintain the Public Revenue, and they must become from year to year more burthensome if we shall, by any error of legislation, diminish the power of any great branch of manufacture to contribute to that revenue.

Taking into view, then, the direct and indirect contributions of a ton of American bars, and placing them side by side with a ton of those made in Britain, the producer of the former has not alone been

* I have now before me the transportation account of an establishment within thirty miles of tide-water, and otherwise favorably situated, from which it appears that the actual railroad charge for carriage of materials and iron was, last year, $13 40 per ton.

reduced to an equality with the latter, but to even a worse position, the British producer being now, in effect, *protected against the American one*, whereas, even under the British free trade tariff of 1846, the mere revenue duty gave the latter some slight protection against the former.

In opposition to this it will, however, be said, that British rails cannot now be imported without loss. That is true to-day, because the premium on gold still remains as a slight protection. To whom, however, are the iron producers indebted for it? Is it to the iron consumers? Is it to that greatest of all consumers, the Government—that one which has just decided that *to that premium alone* the producer shall look in all the future for protection against those "wealthy English capitalists," by whom they have so frequently been crushed? It is not; so directly the reverse of this is it, that every branch of that Government is now striving to put down the price of gold, and thus to deprive that greatest of all our manufactures of the little protection that has been left. But recently, as there is the best reason for believing, a proposition has been made to it on the part of these "wealthy capitalists," having specially in view a great reduction in the price of gold; such a reduction as will, if it shall be carried into effect, place the whole iron manufacture, and many other departments of our now so greatly varied industry, entirely at the mercy of the men who "voluntarily incur immense losses in order to destroy foreign competition, and to gain and keep possession of foreign markets." Whether or not that particular proposition, or any other looking in that direction, will be accepted, no one can now venture to predict; but it requires little of the spirit of prophecy to venture on the prediction that if, in the present state of our tariff legislation, any one at all like it shall be accepted, it will bring with it such reduction of the Internal Revenue as must result in bankruptcy of the Government, to be followed by Revolution.

From that Government the iron producer has now, practically, no protection whatsoever. Does he, then, owe to it, in its character of iron consumer, the performance of any act of duty? As it seems to me, he does not. Even in feudal times protection and service went hand in hand together, the right to demand the latter ceasing with the power to afford the former. Admitting, then, the facts to be as I have stated them, are not the iron producers now free for the adoption of whatsoever measures they may see to be required for *self-protection?* That they are so, I fully believe. Still further do I believe, that as men who desire to protect the public revenue, maintain the public credit, and restore the country to a condition of peace and union, and as citizens anxious to free it from the control of foreign agitators who are in every manner seeking the accomplishment of disunion, it is their *duty* to combine together in opposition to the present combination for our subjection, and for the re-establishment of a state of colonial dependence that, should the present effort prove successful, will be more complete than it has been at any period since the Peace of 1783.

So regarding the question that is now to be settled, it is my belief that a sense of duty should prompt the iron producers to address its consumers in the following terms:—

GENTLEMEN :—

Forty years since, notwithstanding our wonderful superabundance of fuel and of ore, the iron manufacture had among us scarcely an existence. The largest furnace in the Union could not produce 1500 tons a year, and the total product of pig metal was under 50,000. In 1828, now but 36 years since, there was passed the first Tariff Act based on the idea that the producers and consumers of food, cloth, and iron constituted one great family, all of whose interests were in perfect harmony, each with every other. To enable the food producer readily to obtain iron, he must have the miner brought near to him, thus to give value to the coal and the iron lying beneath his land. To enable the producer of iron to obtain cloth, it was deemed necessary that the spinner and the weaver should be brought from abroad to eat the food while spinning and weaving the wool. To enable the ship owner to obtain large return freights, it was deemed necessary to secure to the immigrant certain and well-rewarded employment. To enable the proprietor to sell his land, it was deemed necessary to bring the market to his door, and thus relieve him from the oppressive tax of transportation to which he had been so long subjected by the British system. By that tariff all those things were provided for, the entire harmony of all real and permanent interests being thus established. The result exhibited itself in the facts, that before the lapse of a time equal to that of a single presidential term the consumption of cotton and woollen goods had nearly doubled, that of iron nearly trebled, while that of coal had almost tenfold increased. As a consequence of this there was large consumption of tea, coffee, sugar, and other foreign commodities, the public revenue was great, the national treasury was full, and the public debt was in rapid progress towards that entire extinction which occurred in the following presidential term.

The great improvement in the condition of our people which thus was proved, found its base in the great development of the mineral resources of the country. Without power machinery could not be driven, nor without machinery could cloth be made. As a means of securing that development, the consumers of iron had pledged themselves to protect its producers against a foreign combination whose modes of operation are well described in a Report to Parliament, made but a few years since, from which the following is an extract:—

"The laboring classes generally, in the manufacturing districts of this country and especially in the iron and coal districts, are very little aware of the extent to which they are often indebted for their being employed at all to the immense *losses* which their employers voluntarily incur in bad times, in order *to destroy foreign competition, and to gain and keep possession of foreign markets.* Authentic instances are well known of employers having in such times carried on their works at a loss amounting in the aggregate to three or four hundred thousand pounds in the course of three or four years. If the efforts of those who encourage the combinations to restrict the amount of labor and to produce strikes were to be successful for any length of time, the great accumulations of capital could no longer be made *which enable a few of the most wealthy capitalists to overwhelm all foreign competition in times of great depression,* and thus to clear the way for the *whole trade* to step in when prices revive, and to carry on a great business before *foreign* capital can again accumulate to such an extent as to be able to establish a competition in prices with any chance of success. *The large capitals of this country are the great instruments of warfare against the competing capital of foreign countries,* and are *the most essential* instruments now remaining by which our manufacturing supremacy can be maintained; the other elements—cheap labor, abundance of raw material, means of communication, and skilled labor—being rapidly in process of being equalized."

That pledge having been accepted, large amounts of capital had been applied to the opening of mines, the building of furnaces and mills, and the construction of the roads and canals required for carrying their products to market, thereby laying the foundation of a coal and iron trade that, had it been permitted to obtain development, would long since have placed the country in a position to become the great exporter of iron and of machinery, and thus to take the place that till then had been occupied by England. That pledge however, unfortunately for the country, was *not* redeemed. Then, as always before, agitation in and out of Congress was resorted to for the purpose of striking down this great and fundamental industry, and thus relieving the "wealthy English capitalists" from all danger of future interference. As a consequence of this railroad bars were made free of duty in 1832, and thus were furnaces deprived of the great market opening in that direction for their products. Next, and in the following year, the whole tariff was subjected to a process by means of which iron and all the manufactures in which it was required were speedily to be deprived of all protection. Confidence in the future now wholly passed away. Mills and furnaces ceased to be built. Financial crises followed closely one upon another, with the necessary result of almost annihilating the value of the vast capital, counting by tens of millions, that had been applied to the development of the two great industries upon which then depended the whole future of the Union. It was a destruction of property till then without a parallel in history, to have been accomplished by the act of the very people who were destined most to suffer under it—the producers of food and the consumers of iron. The one lost his market among the men who mined the coal and ore and made the iron, and the other found that the impoverished farmer was unable to buy cloth. In crushing out these two great industries the iron consumers, your predecessors, had, Samson like, torn down the pillars of the Temple, and had involved themselves and their Governments, Municipal, State, and Federal, in one common ruin. Railroads, constructed by aid of *cheap* and worthless British iron made from a long accumulation of cinder, fell so much in value that their proprietors were unable to sell their shares at any price. Workshops were closed, and workmen were everywhere reduced to ask for alms. Spinners and weavers shared the same sad fate with the miner and the founder. The trader, unable to collect the moneys due him, was unable to pay the bank, and the banker followed him in stopping payment of his debts. The National Treasury, reduced to bankruptcy, was unable to borrow, on any terms, the amount required to make amends for the deficiency thus produced in its then trivial revenue. Chaos had come again—the same chaotic state of things that had preceded the passage of the Protective Act of 1824. It had come, too, as a consequence of the inauguration of a government of foreign traders who sought monopoly, and talked of freedom of trade. How free it was, has been shown in the passage from the Parliamentary Report we have above submitted to your consideration. How profitable it had been, was proved by the fact, that, notwithstanding an increase of one-fourth in population, the consumption of iron had scarcely at all increased.

For all this a remedy needed to be found. It came in the form of the tariff of 1842, by which the American people once again pledged themselves to the capitalist, that if he would apply his means to the development of those great mineral resources of the country which constituted the foundation upon which, *alone*, could rest securely our social edifice, he should be protected against those "wealthy capitalists" who had so long been accustomed to regard temporary losses as merely a mode of employing their great "instrument of warfare" in the manner most efficient for the accomplishing of the one great purpose, that of "destroying foreign competition and gaining and keeping possession of foreign markets." The pledge thus tendered was accepted, and in a period brief almost beyond belief mines were opened, roads were constructed, and furnaces and mills were built, capable of supplying a consumption thrice as great as had been that of 1842. With that increase in quantity came such improvements and economies in the mode of manufacture as rendered it absolutely certain that, if faith should be kept with the men who had thus given time, mind, and means to the most important of all manufactures, but a brief period would be required to elapse before they should be enabled to supply the outside world with iron, and thus to furnish new evidence that protection was the road that led most certainly in the direction of perfect freedom of trade. At no period in our history had the demand for labor been so great. At none had there been even an approach to the number of immigrants who then sought our shores. At none had property commanded so large a price. At none had public and private credit been so complete; and yet, but five years previously, labor had been everywhere in excess; immigration had tended to die away; property had been wholly unsaleable; bankruptcy had been almost universal; and the public treasury had found itself wholly unable to command the means required for compliance with its engagements.

As before, however, the public faith was violated, and because of agitation caused by British agents. Almost without notice the pledge given in 1842 was withdrawn in 1846, and the men who in full reliance upon it had applied their millions and tens of millions to carrying in effect the public will in reference to the great work of internal development, were once more delivered over, bound hand and foot, to the "tender mercies of the wealthy capitalists" of England; the men who, while engaged in the work of "overwhelming all foreign competition," could afford to dispense with interest on their capital, their competitors meanwhile paying 10, 15, or 20 per cent. per annum for the use of the money required for carrying stocks constantly accumulating on their hands while engaged in the effort at maintaining the unequal contest.

Further even than all this, the Government undertook to furnish to the foreign producer storage, and under such circumstances as rendered an iron certificate of deposit equally transferable with a money one; whereas, the domestic producer was by law deprived of all modes of transfer not accompanied by an actual delivery of the property itself. The great iron consumer of the country had thus, after having pledged itself to the men who had built the furnaces and rolling mills, opened the mines, and constructed the roads, to protect them in their efforts for the establishment of competition, for the *sale* of iron, entered into an alliance, offensive and defensive, with parties whose essential object was that of destroying all *that* competition, thereby increasing competition for the *purchase* of British iron.

Such a course of policy could have but one result. One by one iron masters succumbed to the pressure. One by one the miners of coal found themselves obliged to abandon their works. Seeing ruin ahead they begged of Congress to give them such a sliding scale as should secure them $50 a ton for sound American iron, twice more useful than the worthless trash that was then being forced upon the markets at $40 by their British competitors. Trifling as was this request it was refused, although but four years before Mr. Calhoun had said, that if he could be assured that American iron masters could supply the market at $80 they should have any amount of protection they saw fit to ask.

American production had now fallen to little more than one-half the amount at which it had stood on the day in which the British iron masters' tariff, that of 1846, had gone into practical effect.

Soon, however, came the influx of California gold, bringing with it a large demand for iron, to be supplied, to a great extent, by foreigners, at whose instance that tariff had been made, and now arose a competition for the *purchase* of their products by which they largely profited, charging double price for all they furnished. In three years they sold in the American market a million of tons of iron in its various forms, and at prices that must have paid twenty times over for the losses "voluntarily incurred" in the years from 1848 to 1850. A hundred millions of dollars of American property had been thrown idle, even where not destroyed, to enable foreign iron masters to tax our people, *in increased prices alone*, a sum little short of that amount. In the decade ending June, 1857, there were imported into the country hundreds of millions of dollars' worth that would have been made at home but for the gross violation, at its outset, of pledges voluntarily given by the ruined and broken-down iron consumers of 1842. In that decade there had been forced upon the English market millions upon millions of dollars' worth of food that ought to have been consumed at home, each successive increase of export tending to lessen the prices of the great regulating market of the world, and thus reducing, to the extent of *thousands of millions of dollars*, the amount yielded to our farmers by their crops.* In this manner was built up the great foreign debt that paved the way for that terrific crisis of 1857, which resulted in the stoppage of merchants, the ruin of manufacturers, the closing of mills, furnaces, and mines, and the depletion of the National Treasury, and thus furnished new and more convincing proof that in the coal and iron of the country were to be found THE PILLARS OF OUR NATIONAL TEMPLE, and that when they are being torn away the destruction of the entire edifice is close at hand.

To those two great interests the whole period from 1856 to 1860—that which succeeded the first excitement consequent upon the dis-

* Every additional bushel of wheat thrown on the British market tends to lower the prices there. Every reduction there is followed by a similar reduction here, as Liverpool prices regulate those of New York, which regulates Chicago. The reduction, therefore, is felt on *the whole crop*. It would be a very small allowance for the reduction of British prices consequent upon American supplies to put it at a shilling—24 cents—per bushel. This upon 1250 millions of bushels would give a loss to American farmers of $300,000,000 a year. This is a large sum, and yet it is short of the truth.

covery of California gold—had been one of constantly recurring crises, ending in the ruin of a large proportion of the people who had given time, mind, and means to their development. To the country at large it had given prostration so complete that, notwithstanding an increase of population to the extent of full two-fifths, the power of our people at its close to make demand for iron was scarcely greater than it had been when the British iron master's tariff of 1846 first became instinct with life and prepared to exert its power for mischief. What was its extent shall now be shown.

Fifteen years before, the power of the Alliance between British free trade and slavery which was now seeking the perpetuation of the Colonial System, had exhibited itself in an attempt at Nullification. Ten years later it had presented itself in the form of an almost entire annihilation of our domestic commerce, and in bankruptcy so general that it included individuals and banks, State and Federal Governments. This time it exhibited itself in a deliberate attempt at destruction of the Union. Throughout the whole of the period that had then elapsed since Carolina had abandoned protection and readopted that system which looked to the confinement of our people to the raising of raw products for distant markets—the system of slavery and barbarism—Liverpool had been becoming daily more and more the centre round which revolved our whole societary system. The men of the West exchanged with those of the East, and those of the South with those of the North, through British traders—through those very men now who since have been devoting all their means and all their influence to the final achievement of the one great end they so long had had in view, the dissolution of the Union. The more they could destroy the domestic commerce the smaller must become the threads by means of which its several sections still continued to be held together. By shutting up the mines, furnaces, and mills of the North they compelled the South to look to them for iron, and the greater the dependence thus produced the higher was necessarily the cost of machinery, and the rate of interest, at the North, with constant increase in Southern dependence on Britain for a market for its cotton. British free trade was thus but the necessary preparation for that movement of 1860 which gave us a war in the course of which rebellion has had all the aid, material and moral, that British traders could give to it. Fomenters of discord during the whole period to which we have referred, they have now labored for its perpetuation.

That war had, however, brought with it a remedy for our evils, for it had, by reason of the secession of Southern Senators, given to the people of the loyal States a power for self-protection of which they had been long denied. The necessity for a re-invigoration of the domestic commerce had now become so very evident that once more there was given to the men of capital *a pledge* that if they would apply their resources to the development of the great mineral resources of the country they should now be certainly protected against the foreigners by whom American competition for the *sale* of iron has been so often and so almost thoroughly destroyed. Past experience was adverse to the acceptance of such a pledge, faith having been so often broken that confidence in the national honor had well nigh disappeared. Nevertheless, it was accepted, and forthwith commenced a forward movement the rapidity of which can find no parallel in the whole history of national development here or elsewhere. But three years have now elapsed since the country first began to recover from the first great shock of civil war, and yet brief as has been the period we are already enabled to show—

I. That the production of pig metal has now attained an amount exceeding 1,300,000 tons; and with so great a development of resources in regard to both fuel and ores that we are warranted in saying, that large as is that quantity, it can be thrice increased in the next four years:

II. That there now exists machinery for the conversion of iron into bars, and into steel, fully capable of supplying the whole present demand, accompanied with a power of increase to an extent equal to any future demand that you, consumers of iron, can, by any possibility, make:

III. That the value of the product of the mines, furnaces, and mills engaged in furnishing coal and iron now exceeds two hundred and fifty millions of dollars, nearly all of which is given to the payment of labor employed in the extraction of coal and ore, in the conversion of the two into the iron that you so greatly need, or in the extension of preparations for the supply of both:

IV. That by thus making demand for labor they are offering large bounties for the importation of men who come here to eat American food while mining coal or ore, building houses or ships, constructing machinery of transportation and manufacture by means of which value is given to land, or farms on which they and their children may raise the food required by other immigrants who follow in their footsteps :

V. That the market for food that, directly or indirectly, is thus *annually* made for the produce of the farm, by these two great branches of industry, is therefore greater in amount than was the total export thereof to Europe in the whole fourteen years from the commencement of vitality in the British Iron Masters' Tariff of 1846 to the breaking out of the rebellion of which that tariff has proved to be the cause:

VI. That, at the lowest estimate, the contributions to the internal revenue, State and national, consequent upon the creation of this immense market for food and labor, and the increased value given to labor, land, and their products, must be taken at eighty millions of dollars; and—

VII. That, notwithstanding the heavy burthens that have been laid on this great industry, notwithstanding the extraordinary increase in the price of labor of all descriptions, and notwithstanding the reduction of the American producer to a level, so far as protection goes, with his British competitor, the latter is even now so far undersold in our own market that American furnaces and rolling-mills supply the whole American demand.

That *our* duty has been performed, and that all the pledges which may have been given for us have been redeemed, are facts of which we thus furnish evidence that cannot be questioned. Has that of the nation been performed? *Has it kept faith with us?* Has *it* redeemed the pledge of protection given at the time when, in the day of its distress, it invited us to devote our lives, and give our time, our mind, and our means towards the re-establishment of that competition with British iron masters for the *sale* of iron which, under the blighting influence of the British free trade tariffs of 1846 and 1857, had so nearly disappeared? Let us inquire.

In March, 1861, before the imposition of any internal tax whatsoever, the protection to be given to railroad bars was fixed at $12 per ton, and it was then well understood to be the very least that could with propriety be accepted by the parties who were thus to be invited to engage in that important and expensive work.

A year later, heavy taxes having been imposed on many articles used in manufactures generally, there was granted to all of them, with the single exception of railroad bars, an additional five per cent. On that one excepted commodity, which now makes demand for nearly 500,000 tons of pig metal, the increase was limited to the exact amount of the direct tax, $1 50 per ton, no allowance having been made, as in other cases, for the taxes on coal, lime, or other materials, nor for many others, including that on incomes. We have here the first violation of the pledge given in 1861.

At the last session of Congress, pig-iron was taxed $2 per ton, equivalent to nearly $3 on a ton of bars. The taxes on coal and other materials were largely increased. That on railroad iron itself was more than doubled. Others were imposed too numerous here to recapitulate—the general result being, that our various contributions, consequent upon the existence of the war, have now been carried up to $10 per ton. Was the duty on foreign iron correspondingly increased? Was the pledge given in 1861 now redeemed? On the contrary, such was the agitation on the part of many of you, gentlemen, consumers of iron, urged thereto by British emissaries, that the duty on foreign iron was *reduced to exactly the point at which it had stood when domestic iron had been free from all such charges.* Thus for the second time was the national faith violated, and this time on so grand a scale that we find ourselves now placed in a position, as compared with the foreigner, worse than was that we occupied under the ultra free trade tariff of 1857. Then, *we* had some slight protection. Now, the foreigner, as we shall show, is *protected against us.*

Before doing this we must, however, consider the present transient protection resulting from the fact that the cost of British iron, and the duties on it, must be paid in gold, the premium thereon being all that now remains to us as offset against a duplication, even where not a triplication, of the cost of labor and its products. No part of that, however, do we hold because of any exercise of power by Government, from which we yet hold the pledge given in 1861, now waiting to be redeemed. So far the reverse of this is it, that time and again has its Finance Minister given his best efforts for the removal of the only protection thus left to us. Time and again has it listened to proposals for its removal coming from foreigners who see therein the only remaining bar to the flooding of our markets with the produce of foreign mines, mills, and furnaces. Time and again have there been, on the part of Congress, efforts at movement in that direction. Time and again have we been assured by leading Republican journals that with any increase in the prospect of peace there must be a growing tendency towards the breaking down of that only barrier which stands between the great fundamental industries of the country and utter ruin. The great iron consumer spares no effort for the accomplishment of that object, and therein all the lesser consumers unite with it heart and hand. Busily as the paper consumers are employed in striking from under their feet that great branch of manufacture which furnishes the foundation on which they stand, even more so are you, gentlemen, iron consumers, engaged in undermining the foundations on which now stand the paper-maker and the printer, the spinner and the weaver, the ship-owner and the railroad proprietor, the machinist and the architect, the city and the county revenues, the State and Federal Governments. All of these, large consumers of iron, are now anxiously awaiting the time when, to the already violated faith of the Union there shall be added that conversion into gold of the taxes that have been so *heaped up* on us—graduated as they had been by a paper standard—which shall, when connected with public storage, place the foreign producer in the enviable position of being PROTECTED BY THE AMERICAN GOVERNMENT AGAINST THE AMERICAN IRON MASTER. All of them seem to be of the belief that by thus annihilating American competition for the *sale* of iron and increasing American competition for the *purchase* of British iron their demands must be more cheaply supplied. All of them have forgotten the lesson taught by the repeated crises of the British free trade tariffs of 1816, 1833, 1846, and 1857. All of them, finally, seem to be of the opinion that when the foundation upon which now rests our whole social system shall have been removed, the edifice will yet remain unharmed. It is a sad delusion, but as it exists we find ourselves required to look it fully in the face and determine what it is that our duty to our country and to ourselves requires us to do in the state of things that has been produced.

With the restoration of peace there will arise a demand for labor throughout the South that must tend greatly to prevent any material decrease in its price throughout the North. Tobacco and cotton fields will thus become competitors with the furnaces, mills, factories, and other establishments now in existence, and these latter must for a considerable period of time be compelled to choose between paying high wages, on the one hand, and closing their works on the other. The present rate of wages in the coal and iron trades is little less than treble that of England, and how little the latter

6

can be expected to rise is shown by the facts, that the Scottish miners, at the close of a turn out, on which they expended all their means to the extent of $7,500,000, have recently been obliged to give in and return to work under the wages against which they had rebelled; and, that the very latest *Iron Trade Circular* (Birmingham) advises its readers, that "the present state of the iron trade in all parts of the country, both in North and South Staffordshire, South Wales, and the Cleveland districts, justifies, or rather we should say, forces their masters to call upon the men for a reduction of wages." Such being the case, it is clear that it is not in that direction we can look for any change by which we might hope to profit. Further even than this, British wages must rise so soon as the "wealthy English capitalists" shall have had the way opened to them for crushing out American competition, and then immigration must, as we feel assured, fall to a point lower than any it has touched since the terrific crisis of 1842. In that direction, then, we cannot look for help.

Taxes *must* be maintained at the present standard should that continue practicable. Further, indeed, than this, they must, wherever possible, be increased, as the nominal amount of business declines with the decline of prices. Incomes will count far less in gold than they now do in paper. Sales will do the same, and the gold received, admitting the quantity of goods sold even to remain the same, will be one-half less than that now received in paper. The interest on the debt will remain undiminished. So, too, must it be with soldiers' and sailors' wages, and the salaries of officers, civil, military, and naval—all of whom will then be enabled to purchase twice the quantity of commodities they can now command. Looking at all these facts, it seems to us to be quite clear that to meet the demands of the Government it will be needed that, wherever possible, the taxes shall be raised. That they cannot be reduced is absolutely certain.

Labor, for a time at least, remaining unchanged, and taxes continuing to be collected on coal, oil, &c. &c., the cost of all the materials of iron must continue to be so high as to afford to the iron master only the choice between closing his works, on the one hand, and ruin on the other. Transportation, the charge for which has now been carried up to a point so terrific, will remain for a time unchanged. Railroad companies, having tasted the sweets of such high charges, will certainly try the experiment of breaking their customers before they abandon them.

Interest must rise as bank loans decline in their amount. In all past crises it has been from three to six times higher than has been paid by "wealthy English capitalists" when they have been compelled to carry heavy stocks of iron.

Taking all these things together we think it quite safe to say that, for the first year at least, the cost to the American iron master of producing and transporting a ton of bars will be greater by *twenty dollars* than will be that of a ton produced in England at the present low rate of wages. Against this there will be a difference of *two dollars* in the taxes. The protection of the "wealthy English capitalist" will be complete, but where then will stand those American rivals who have now so completely occupied the domestic market as to have greatly reduced English wages, and thus paved the way for immigration from the British soil of tens of thousands of her workers in coal and iron, whose services have so much been needed? Once here, they and their children would forever be customers to the farmers of the Mississippi Valley. Forced to remain where they are they will, as heretofore, eat the food of Russia or of Egypt. That they *will not* come under a system that protects the British capitalist against his American competitor is very certain. The importation of such machinery, capable of making engines, while reproducing themselves, *of the past year*, is worth more to the country than all the iron that has ever come to it from British furnaces since the unfortunate repeal, under Carolinian threats of secession, of the protective tariff of 1828.

Such being the existing state of facts, and such the prospects, we have now to determine what we ourselves should do. To attempt, under such circumstances, to maintain a competition for the *sale* of iron, could result only in a gradual depletion of every ironmaster in the country, and in the abandonment of his works after he should himself have been ruined. The day of high prices would then come round again, but there would exist no person to profit of it. By withdrawing at once, before the day of exhaustion had commenced, we should, on the contrary, retain ourselves in a position to resume work when the day should have arrived for giving a new pledge of the faith that has been so often, and, as we think, so discreditably violated. By adopting this latter course, we should retain the power to aid in the re-establishment of that internal commerce upon which the country is now so entirely dependent for the power to maintain the Government. By pursuing the former, we should speedily place ourselves in a condition to require aid, instead of granting it. After full consideration, therefore, we have arrived at the conclusion that we should best perform our duty, both public and private, by withdrawing from competition with those "wealthy English capitalists" who are now so anxious to sell cheap iron, and who have always doubled their prices so soon as they had annihilated their American competitors. You will, therefore, please to receive this as a notice that from and after the first of March next our works will be closed, and you will be free to make such arrangements in regard to the supply of iron as best may suit your convenience.

Should, in the mean time, any of you be disposed to commence the work of producing iron that is to pay nearly as much in taxes as the foreign product pays in the form of duties, you can, as we think, be supplied with any number of furnaces and mills at their actual cost, and in very many cases at less than cost.

Yours, respectfully, A. B.
C. D.
E. F.

Such, as it appears to me, is the course that duty requires of the ironmasters of the country to pursue. Past experience proves that there can be no reliance on the pledges given to them when the country needs their aid. Foreign emissaries haunt the halls of Congress, and their presence there is not alone tolerated, but actually courted, by gentlemen who can see advantage in enabling a constituent to save a dollar or two upon a few thousand tons of iron, and who cannot see that the power to buy iron at any price has resulted from American competition for the *purchase* of the products of the farm, and for the *sale* of those yielded by the mine, the furnace, and the rolling-mill. It is time, therefore, that they should now abandon the position they so long have occupied, that of supplicants for mercy, and, as the best mode of serving the country, maintaining its revenue, and thus enabling its Government to live, take at once the true ground that, in ceasing to grant protection, the iron consumers have lost all claim upon them for the performance of duties.

It may perhaps be charged that this would be combination. It would be so, and the time has come for it. The country has now to carry on a war with foreign capitalists and their agents, for the maintenance of its credit, for the perpetuation of the Union, and for the conversion of the Declaration of Independence into something more than a mere form of words, and it will be worsted if the honest people of the country do not combine for its support. By so doing, they will speedily be enabled to obtain from foreign nations indemnity for the past and security for the future, for in that combination they will be sure to find *the way to outdo England without fighting her.*

To enable ourselves to succeed we need only that stability of action which shall give to the capitalists security against foreign agitation. But a few days since one of the largest importers of British iron expressed to one of my friends a wish that Congress should take such decided action as would warrant him in turning his capital from the importation to the production of this most important commodity, the materials of which so much abound throughout the Union. Let it but do this and the day will then be close at hand when the annual production will count by millions of tons, and when our farmers will be relieved of all necessity for crushing down, in the regulating market of the world, the prices of all their products. The *annual* saving thereby produced would be greater in its amount than the value of all the iron imported into the country since the Peace of Ghent.

In my next I shall ask your attention to the Farmer's Question; meanwhile, my dear sir, remaining,

Yours, very truly,

HENRY C. CAREY.

Hon. SCHUYLER COLFAX.

PHILADELPHIA, January 16, 1865.

THE FARMER'S QUESTION.

LETTER NINTH.

DEAR SIR :—

IN a former letter the money value of the products of our coal and iron mines, our furnaces and rolling-mills, was stated as being little less than two hundred and fifty millions. Following that iron through the foundries and machine shops we shall find that those industries are this day yielding to the nation commodities whose market value certainly exceeds *four hundred millions ;* and then following their proceeds we find that nearly the whole is distributed among the men who own the land and those who cultivate it. Hence it is, that whenever those two great industries prosper the farmer prospers ; and that when they suffer he too becomes a heavy sufferer.

Are the facts so ? it may here be asked. *Are* their proceeds so applied ? Let us see.

Of this vast sum a very large proportion is distributed among the men who mine our coal and ore—men who aid in transporting them—men who aid in converting the two into iron—men who puddle the iron and roll the bar—and other men who convert the bar into hoes, spades, axes, knives, and engines. What becomes of it then ? They buy food for their families and themselves, all of which comes from American farmers. They purchase clothing made of Western wool or Southern cotton, and converted by means of men and women who tend the spindle and the loom while eating the food of Iowa and Minnesota. They buy houses composed of bricks and lumber, the one made, and the other cut and brought to market, by men who eat the pork of Ohio and the corn of Indiana or of Illinois. They buy newspapers whose types and paper represent the hams of Kentucky, the wheat of Pennsylvania, and the butter and cheese of New York, while its press represents the food consumed in workshops which, in the wonderful character of the machines turned out, furnish to the world such conclusive proof that were American farmers but true to themselves American ingenuity would speedily relieve them from the necessity for employing themselves in raising food for distant markets, the proper work of the barbarian and the slave, *and of them alone.*

A part of this vast sum goes, however, to the owners of land that yields coal, ore, or lime; another, to those who own furnaces, in which the three are converted into iron, or shops in which iron is converted into machinery to be used by the farmer, the weaver, the locomotive builder, and the builder of ships; and we may now inquire what becomes of *them.* These men have families, and those families likewise need food that comes from American farms; clothing all of which, were our farmers true to themselves, would represent the products of American agriculture; houses which represent the labors of brickmakers and bricklayers, lumbermen, carpenters, masons, workers in coal, and workers in iron, all of them men who help to make the great market in which exchanges of food to the annual extent of thousands of millions of dollars are now made. The profits of some of the owners of the great works from which are now annually turned out so many millions of tons of coal, so many hundreds of thousands of tons of iron, and so many engines, are, however, as we know, greatly in excess of their expenditure. What becomes of the surplus? A part of it is applied to the extension of their works, and thus is created demand for labor, enabling many to obtain food and clothing who otherwise might be unemployed and therefore unable to purchase either. Another part goes to the making of railroads, thus creating a further demand for labor, and giving the farmer a purchaser for his pork and his corn while at the same time increasing his facilities for reaching the distant markets. Another part, perhaps, is lent to the Government, and thus aids it in paying the farmer for the food, the clothing, and the machinery required by our armies in the field. Thus, of the whole five hundred millions, large as is the sum, it may, as I believe, be safely assumed that more than ninety per cent., and perhaps even ninety-five, goes directly, or indirectly, to the payment of labor that is employed in clearing and cultivating the land.

Turning now back to the period of the British free trade tariffs of 1846 and 1857, we see that hundreds of millions worth of foreign iron had been imported—part of it in the form of knives and razors, very much of it in that of mere pig metal, and hundreds of thousands of tons in that of rails to be laid on lands the larger part of which abounded in fuel and in ore waiting alone the application of labor to their extraction and conversion. Why was this? Because the system of that day had been framed in obedience to orders issued by the men who since have been employed in building pirate ships to be used in driving from the ocean the stars and stripes; in fitting out other ships for running our blockade; and generally in giving to the rebellion that aid, material and moral, by help of which a war that should have been finished in a year has been prolonged throughout a whole Presidential term, and at a cost of hundreds of lives and hundreds of millions of property that might otherwise have been saved.

For the iron thus imported we have paid hundreds of millions of dollars. What became of *them?* Did the people who mined the coal and the ore employed in making *that* iron eat American wheat? Did *they* wear clothing composed of corn raised in Iowa and wool sheared in Ohio? Did *they* occupy houses built with lumber representing the food of Michigan or Minnesota? Did the workmen who built the houses *they* occupied consume potatoes raised in Maine, or cabbages raised in Pennsylvania? For an answer to these questions I give you the following figures representing the wheat, the wool, the flour, the pork, and the lumber exported—not alone to the country from which we had the iron, but to France, Belgium, and Great Britain, the countries which have deluged us with the silks, the woollens, the cottons, and the iron by means of the purchase of which we have been involved in a foreign debt of $500,000,000 that now makes upon us, *for the mere payment of interest,* a demand to meet which requires not less than $30,000,000, a sum more than half the product of California. The years I have taken are the three which immediately preceded the breaking out of the great rebellion. The country had then for more than a decade enjoyed the *blessings* of that British free trade which, as we were assured in 1847, was destined, before the lapse of twenty years, to make a demand for American food whose *annual* amount would count by hundreds of millions of dollars. To what extent those predictions have been realized will be seen by the following figures:—

	Total Export.	To Great Britain, France, and Belgium.
1858.		
Pork	$2,852,492	$360,000
Indian corn . . .	3,259,039	2,163,000
Lumber . . .	1,240,000	215,000
Wheat	9,061,000	6,436,000
Wheat flour . . .	19,328,884	5,006,000
Wool	389,512	15,000
1859.		
Pork	3,355,746	563,000
Indian corn . . .	1,323,103	281,000
Lumber . . .	1,001,216	247,000
Wheat	2,849,192	1,402,000
Wheat flour . . .	14,493,591	1,147,000
Wool	355,563	129,000
1860.		
Pork	2,852,942	371,000
Indian corn . . .	3,259,039	1,894,000
Lumber . . .	1,240,425	475,000
Wheat	9,061,504	6,389,000
Wheat flour . . .	19,328,880	5,133,000
Wool	211,861	141,000
Total	$95,463,989	$32,367,000
Annual average .	31,821,330	10,789,000

The annual average, as here is shown, of the demand for these important commodities by the three great manufacturing countries of Europe, was less than $11,000,000, or little more than 16 cents per head of their total population. A single hundred thousand of their people attracted here by large demand for labor and liberal wages, would furnish a market for the various products of the land much greater in its amount.

The great European market for food that had been promised to our farmers had, as we see, totally failed. Had the deficiency of demand thus produced been in any manner made up by immigration? On the contrary, the number of foreigners coming here to sell their labor was less in those years, as has been shown in a former letter —less, too, by thirty per cent.—than it had been in the year in which the British iron master's tariff of 1846 first became endued with power for mischief.

Under the free trade tariff of 1841–2 the markets furnished by the coal and iron industries of the country could but little have exceeded $50,000,000. Under the protective tariff act of 1842, that market thrice increased in size, having, in less than half a dozen years, grown to $150,000,000. In the same time immigration had also thrice increased, and as every immigrant became a consumer on the moment of his arrival, whereas one year at least must elapse before any one of them could make the slightest addition to the quantity of food produced, *it followed that to the whole extent of their consumption of food, of wool, of cotton, of lumber, and of all other of the products of the land, they constituted an addition to the farmer's market.* Admitting that their average power to earn wages amounted to but $150 a year, the addition amounted to $25,000,000. The movement had, however, then only just commenced. The more iron made in 1846 the greater was the quantity required in 1847; and the more made in this latter year the greater would have been the quantity required in 1848, '49, and '50; and the greater the immigration of 1847 the more would have been its tendency to increase in each and every of the succeeding years, had protection been maintained. Had it been so, our coal and iron industries would this day amount to more than $1,000,000,000, making demand to nearly the whole of that vast amount for the fruits of the earth, while immigration would by this time have been giving us a million per annum of European workmen, consumers, from the moment of their arrival, of the products of American farms, and busily engaged in the work of further increasing by procreation the number of mouths requiring further supplies of food and wool.

We were told, however, that iron masters were too rapidly growing rich; that the taxes imposed for their benefit on iron consumers were so great that they amounted to more than the whole price at which their finished products could be bought; that the farmers were thus made mere "hewers of wood and drawers of water" for great monopolists; that protection closed the markets of Europe against their "breadstuffs;" that we were essentially an agricultural people, and so likely to remain; that we therefore needed free trade; and that, for all these reasons, the protection should be abandoned. It *was* abandoned, and we have now the result in the facts, that we had given up a domestic market among the producers of coal, iron, copper, lead, and cloth, which then amounted to hundreds of millions, and would since then have arrived at thousands of millions, and had, at the close of the system inaugurated in its stead, obtained in exchange a market which took from us of pork, corn, wheat, flour, wool, and lumber, less than $11,000,000 a year, *or one-third of a dollar per head of our then population.* Such had been the results obtained in 1860 by means of agitation on the part of those British agents by whom had been represented in 1846, in the Halls of the Capitol, those wealthy capitalists of England whose first desire was that food might be obtained more cheaply while iron should command a higher price.

Did *they* obtain their end? To obtain an answer to this question we may here compare the prices in the New York market at the commencement and the close of that period of the British free trade system which dates from December, 1846. As given in a table now before me, they are as follows:—

	1847.	1858.	1859.	1860.
Wheat flour . . .	7 68	4·25	5 50	5 50
Rye flour . . .	5 06	3 40	3 75	3 50
Corn meal . . .	4 62	3 50	3 90	3 80
Pork	14 93	18 35	16 35	17 75
Mess Beef . . .	12 00	11 50	8 25	5 25
Butter . . .	25	25	22½	18

In the period intervening between the first and last of these dates, California and Australia had given to the world probably $800,000,000 in gold, and yet, instead of increasing as it should have done, the power of the farmer to obtain money in exchange for his products had largely diminished.

The reason for this was to be found in the fact, that determining to go abroad to get his iron and his cloth he had destroyed his great market. To what extent this had been done you may, my dear sir, judge for yourself after referring to an extract from an Address of one of the Charitable Societies of New York, given in a former letter, but here reproduced because of its important bearing on the question now before us:—

"Up to the present the Association has relieved 6,922 families, containing 26,896 persons, *many of whom are families of unemployed mechanics* and widows with dependent children, who cannot subsist without aid. As the season advances the destitution will increase. Last winter it was thrice as great in January as in December, and did not reach its height until the close of February."

This paper bears date more than a year previous to the great crisis of 1857. Subsequently thereto the state of things was very far worse than that above described. Our public warehouses were filled with foreign merchandise, always ready to supply the material of auction sales. Our auctioneers, constantly at work, supplied wholesale and retail dealers, at prices fixed by themselves. Our shops were gorged so thoroughly with foreign food and labor in every form, from the coarsest woollens to the finest silks, as to leave no place for the domestic food and labor that sought a market. Such was the mode of "warfare," by means of which "*the most wealthy capitalists*" of Britain *had been enabled to* "*overwhelm all foreign competition in times of great depression, and thus to clear the way for the whole trade to step in, when prices revived, and to carry on a great business, before foreign capital could accumulate to such an extent as to be able to establish a competition in prices with any chance of success.*" Such, my dear sir, was the sort of warfare, by means of which Ireland and India had been ruined, without the necessity for firing a gun, or drawing a sword. Such was the warfare against which your fellow-citizens, for ten years previously, had sought, but vainly sought, to be protected—the only answer to the petitions having been, that the duties of the government were limited to the task of protecting itself, leaving the people to protect themselves as best they could.

As a consequence of this it was: that after a growth of pauperism steadily continued during all those years, it suddenly so much expanded that hundreds of thousands of our people were wholly unable to sell their labor, or to purchase food and clothing:

The factories, mills, mines, and furnaces, the cost of which had counted by hundreds of millions of dollars, were then closed, and likely so to remain:

That the power to diversify the employments of society was then declining from day to day:

That, simultaneously therewith, we were adding to our population a million of persons annually:

That the necessity for resorting to the labors of the field, as affording the only means of support, was steadily increasing:

That the supply of food tended, therefore, to augment, as the domestic consumption declined: and

That its price tended, therefore, steadily to fall, and was, at the outset of the war, likely to be lower than had ever yet been known.

The production of iron had largely decreased, as under such

circumstances might readily be supposed. What, however, was its import? Did the figures there presented furnish any evidence of increase of power on the part of the farmer to purchase hoes or ploughs, or on that of the miner to purchase engines? Let us see.

In the three years above referred to there was imported of iron and manufactures of iron, to the extent of $45,000,000, giving an annual average of $15,000,000, or *less than fifty cents per head of our population.* In the hope to secure some trifling reduction in its price our farmer had been persuaded to throw away a market that then amounted to hundreds of millions, and that would, before 1860, have reached thousands of millions, and now the whole amount taken from him of his chief products, by the three principal manufacturing nations of Europe, was barely sufficient to pay for the little iron that he could afford to purchase and the freight upon it; that freight, too, paid chiefly for the use of British ships. As a necessary consequence, the country was running in debt from day to day more deeply, and the interest on that debt was even then absorbing more than half the gold yielded by California. Hence it had been that the prices of the farmer's products had fallen in price as the supplies of the precious metals had so rapidly increased. Busily engaged in selling *skins* at sixpence each, and taking pay therefor in *tails* at a shilling, he had been giving all his efforts at increasing the power of that great combination of "wealthy English capitalists," the primary object of all whose operations had been that of depressing the prices of food and raising the price of iron—diminishing still further that of the skins and raising still higher that of the tails.

The most useful to the British traders of all the British colonies is that one which embraces these United States. Content with the word "independence," Americans take no care to make themselves or their country independent. So far the reverse is it, indeed, that, while talking largely of the Monroe Doctrine, they permit their laws to be dictated to them by British agents, representing ".wealthy capitalists," who now seek to perpetuate throughout this Western Continent the system so well described in the following passage by one of their predecessors of the last century:—

"Manufactures in our American colonies should be discouraged, prohibited." * * "We ought always to keep a watchful eye over our colonies, *to restrain them from setting up any of the manu-*

factures which are carried on in Great Britain; and any such attempts should be crushed in the beginning." * * "Our colonies are much in the same state as Ireland was in, when they began the woollen manufactory, *and as their numbers increase, will fall upon manufactures for clothing themselves, if due care be not taken to find employment for them,* in raising such productions as may enable them to furnish themselves with all the necessaries from us." * * "As they will have the providing rough materials to themselves, so shall we have the manufacturing of them. If encouragement be given for raising hemp, flax, &c., doubtless they will soon begin to manufacture, *if not prevented.* Therefore, *to stop the progress of any such manufacture,* it is proposed that no weaver have liberty to set up any looms, without first registering at an office, kept for that purpose." * * "That all slitting-mills, and engines for drawing wire or weaving stockings, *be put down.*" * * "*That all negroes be prohibited from weaving either linen or woollen, or spinning or combing wool, or working at any manufacture of iron,* further than making it into pig or bar iron. That they also be *prohibited* from manufacturing *hats, stockings, or leather of any kind.* This limitation will not abridge the planters of any liberty they now enjoy—on the contrary, it will then turn their industry to promoting and raising those rough materials." * * "If we examine into the circumstances of the inhabitants of our plantations, and our own, it will appear that *not one-fourth of their product redounds to their own profit, for, out of all that comes here, they only carry back clothing and other accommodations for their families,* all of which is of the merchandise and manufacture of this kingdom." * * "All these advantages we receive by the plantations, *besides the mortgages on the planters' estates and the high interest they pay us, which is very considerable.*"—(GEE *on Trade,* London, 1750.)

A century earlier the Germans had ridiculed the people of England as men who sold skins for sixpence and bought back the tails at a shilling. *Protection* had changed all this. It had brought the English artisan to take his place by the side of the English farmer, and now the English trader desired to do by the American colonist what the German had previously done by him—giving his whole efforts to the work of compelling the sale *to* him of skins at sixpence and the purchase *from* him of tails at a shilling. Thus far they had, with us, most thoroughly succeeded, and had done so by help of the very farmers by means of whose plunder they had obtained the power which recently has been so much increased, and of the exercise of which we have now so much reason to complain.

To that great error on the part of American farmers we have

been indebted for the present war. What are the facts bearing on their present condition and future prospects, that have been developed in its course, and what the measures required for enabling us to *outdo England without fighting her*, and thus achieve an independence that shall be something more than a mere form of words, I propose to show in another letter, meanwhile remaining,

Yours, very truly,

HENRY C. CAREY.

Hon. S. Colfax.

Philadelphia, January 20, 1865.

THE FARMER'S QUESTION.

LETTER TENTH.

DEAR SIR:—

THE period, 1858–60, embraced in the returns given in my last, was one of peace, and much of the food of the West yet continued to pass southward on its way to European markets. Wheat took the form of flour, and corn became pork, for the supply of men engaged in raising and forwarding cotton. The latter went abroad, there to be combined with Polish and Russian wheat, to be thence returned to the poor farmer of Wisconsin who was glad to obtain even a single yard of indifferent cotton cloth in pay for a bushel of corn that had been exchanged in the market of Manchester for fifteen or twenty yards. He was thus giving whole *skins* for sixpence and taking his pay in *tails* at a shilling; as a consequence of which he was always in debt, and always glad to borrow a little money, even when obliged to pay for the use of it at the extraordinary rates of 20, 30, 40, 50, and even, as I have understood, 60 per cent. per annum. Why was this? Not certainly because of any absence of fertility in the soil, that of the Mississippi Valley being equal in all natural powers to any other in the world. Not because, as in Europe, of any necessity for paying rent to a greedy landlord, for he had already attained to the position so much coveted by the working class of Europe, that of landed proprietor. Why then was it? Because he had, of his own motion, made himself the mere *serf* of the class whose operations were so well described in the passage given at the close of my last; of that class which desires that food may be cheap and cloth and iron dear; of that one which seeks to compel all the farmers of the world to bring their products to a single diminutive market, there to sell what they have and to buy what they need; of that one which talks of free trade while seeking to create for itself an absolute monopoly of machinery of conversion and exchange; of that one, in fine, which now stands indebted to him and others like him for all the power which has, in the past four years, been used for the destruction of our commerce on the seas, for the maintenance of the rebellion, and for the annihilation of that Union upon whose prolonged existence is now dependent the whole future of the laboring classes not of America alone, but of the world at large.

The war having closed the South against the products of the West, there arose a necessity for seeking a market somewhere in the East. Where, however, could they have even looked for it, had we continued to maintain that British free trade system under which we had been made so almost entirely dependent upon distant nations for supplies of cloth and iron? Look as they might it could nowhere have been found. Happily, secession brought with it, and on the instant, a power on the part of the North which speedily exhibited itself in the re-adoption of that protective system by means of which the value of the products of our coal and iron mines, our furnaces and rolling mills, has been carried up to two hundred and fifty millions of dollars, making demand, in a thousand ways, for the fruits of the earth to little short of that vast amount. The effect of the creation of this great market exhibits itself in the Message of Governor Yates, of Illinois, just now delivered, the following extract from which is recommended to the careful consideration of the farmers of the country:—

"As a State, notwithstanding the war, we have prospered beyond all former precedents. Notwithstanding nearly two hundred thousand of the most athletic and vigorous of our population have been withdrawn from the field of production, the area of land now under cultivation is greater than at any former period, and the census of 1865 will exhibit an astonishing increase in every department of material industry and advancement; in a great increase of agricultural, manufacturing, and mechanical wealth; in new and improved modes for production of every kind; in the substitution of machinery for the manual labor withdrawn by the war; in the triumphs of invention; in the wonderful increase of railroad enterprise; in the universal activity of business, in all its branches; in the rapid growth of our cities and villages; in the bountiful harvests, and in an unexampled material prosperity, prevailing on every hand; while, at the same time, the educational institutions of the people have in no way declined. Our colleges and schools, of every class and grade, are in the most flourishing condition; our benevolent institutions, State and private, are kept up and maintained; and, in a word, our prosperity is as complete and ample as though no tread of armies or beat of drum had been heard in all our borders."

It may be said, however, that the Government demand for food has had much to do with the change for the better that is here exhibited. Whence, however, has the National Treasury obtained the means by which it has been enabled to pay its troops and buy their food? Whence have come the vast sums required for fitting out our present enormous fleets? Whence have come those required for constructing roads in Illinois and other Western States? Why is it that the people have been, in time of war, enabled to do so much when in the previous time of peace they could do so very little? For an answer to all these questions, my dear sir, allow me to ask you to look to the following exhibit of the movements of the New York savings banks in the last seven years:—

	No. of Banks.	Amt. of Deposits.	No. of Depositors.
Jan. 1, 1858 . . .	54	$41,422,672	203,804
" 1859 . . .	56	48,194,847	230,074
" 1860 . . .	64	58,178,160	273,697
" 1861 . . .	71	67,440,397	300,693
" 1862 . . .	74	64,083,119	300,511
" 1863 . . .	71	76,538,183	347,184
" 1864 . . .	71	93,786,384	400,194

We have here 400,000 little capitalists, the average of whose savings is but $235, giving us a total of little less than a hundred millions of dollars. Two of those banks are specially devoted to the care of the funds of immigrants, and the following figures exhibit the extent of their operations:—

	Resources.	No. of Depositors.
Jan. 1, 1860	2,442,048	10,360
" 1861	3,420,321	14,838
" 1862	3,471,777	14,365
" 1863	4,475,291	18,621
" 1864	6,056,600	24,151

Turning now to Massachusetts, we find the increase of deposits in the four years, 1860–63, to have been more than a third of the total amount deposited in all the long period that previously had elapsed. The actual increase was $17,503,000, of which no less than $12,150,000 took place in '62 and '63. The mere savings of two States, in two years, thus present us with an increase of capital exceeding $40,000,000, a sum that is one-half as great as that of the whole British capital that, twenty-five years since, had been applied to the building of the mills, workshops, and warehouses, and to the creation of the machinery, required for the then gigantic cotton manufacture.

When furnaces and factories are being increased in number labor is in demand, wages rise, immigration grows, and the power of accumulation increases; and hence it is, that with every step in that direction we witness a manifestation of greater power for further progress. From '58 to '61, notwithstanding a large increase in the number of New York banks, and consequent wide extension of their field of operations, the increase of deposits was but $26,000,000. The first year of the war brought with it a shock that caused suspension of business, accompanied by great decline of wages, and the result, as we see, exhibited itself in a large diminution of deposits. The second year of war brought with it that revival of demand for labor which had always previously attended the re-establishment of protection, and with it came an increase of deposits amounting, in the two succeeding years, to little less than $30,000,000. That increase, too, was obtained without any extension of the field of operations, the number of banks in the last year having been actually less than it had been two years before.

With the increased demand for labor consequent upon the creation of a great domestic market for food the whole country has become one great savings' bank, as a consequence of which the State and Federal Governments have been enabled to collect thousands of millions where before they could scarcely obtain hundreds, the people meanwhile creating for themselves machinery of production and transportation to an extent greater than ever before had been created in the same period of time in any country of the world.*

It may be said, however, that there has been a European demand for our provisions and our bread-stuffs, and such has certainly been the case. Just at the moment when the Southern demand ceased Providence was pleased, in mercy to us, to afflict the people beyond the Atlantic with two successive crops both of which were much below the average, and thus was created one of those unexpected demands for which, under the British free trade system, our far-

* In 1857, there were in operation 26,210 miles of railroad. In 1861, 31,800, giving an average increase of 1,120 miles per annum. Last year there were 35,000, giving an annual increase of 1,067 per annum—that obtained, too, at a time when the demand for services in the mills, mines, and factories of the country, and in the field, had doubled, even where it had not trebled the price of labor.

mers are compelled so fervently and so frequently to pray, though knowing well that short crops abroad must bring famine, distress, and ruin to thousands and tens of thousands of men who, like themselves, have wives and children to support. The momentary effect exhibits itself in the fact that in the three years ending June 30, 1863, our exports of the principal articles of food were as follows:—

	1860–61	1861–62	1862–63
Wheat . . .	$38,313,624	$42,573,295	$31,430,270
Flour . . .	24,645,289	27,534,677	25,458,989
Corn . . .	6,890,865	10,387,383	3,321,526
Pork . . .	2,609,818	3,980,153	4,334,775
Hams and bacon	4,729,297	10,004,521	15,775,570
	$77,188,893	$94,480,029	$80,321,130

What, however, were the prices at which these commodities were given to the European world? What was the great bonus that even then, in times of scarcity, was paid to American farmers in return for closing up in 1846 a market among our miners of coal and iron, lead and copper, that would before that day have amounted to thousands of millions of dollars? Let us see.

As given in the Reports of Commerce and Navigation, the export prices, reckoned for the first year in gold, and for the subsequent ones in paper, were as follows:—

	1860–61	1861–62	1862–63
Wheat, per bushel . . .	$1 22	$1 29	$1 33
Flour, per barrel	5 00	5 70	6 40
Corn, per bushel	62	55	66
Pork, per barrel	17 00	13 00	13 00
Hams, &c., per pound . .	10	8½	10½

Deducting from these prices the heavy charges of transportation and converting the balance into gold it must be clearly seen that it is not in that direction we are to seek the cause of the improvement now observed in the condition of the agricultural population of Illinois and other loyal States. Where then shall it be sought? *In the direction of the production of commodities that do not bear transportation, and that are dependent for a market upon the domestic demand alone.* Read over, my dear sir, the passage above given as descriptive of the condition of Illinois, and you will see that it indicates demand for commodities whose bulk, or whose delicacy, forbids transportation. Potatoes and turnips, of which the earth yields by hundreds of bushels to the acre, cannot be raised where the domestic market has no existence. When, however, the coal mine, the lead mine, or the iron ore mine, comes to be opened, the market is at once created, and it extends itself with every new furnace, every new factory, every new rolling mill, until at length the farmer everywhere obtains the power to determine for himself whether to raise thousands of bushels of potatoes, or hundreds of bushels of wheat; and then it is that the Declaration of Independence becomes to him something more than a mere form of words; then it is that it becomes a reality and a blessing.

That independence, however, is precisely what the "wealthy English capitalist" does not desire that he shall obtain. What *he* desires is, that the distant farmer shall have no market near him; that he shall be compelled to limit himself to the production of commodities of which the earth yields little, and that can, therefore, go to that distant market in which Russian, Polish, German, Egyptian, and American food producers are to contend with each other as to which shall sell most cheaply—then again competing with each other for raising the prices of all the commodities they need to purchase. In this manner it is that *he* buys *skins* at sixpence while selling *tails* at a shilling. By this it is that he is enabled to put into his own pocket three-fourths of the produce of the labor of those poor and distant *serfs* to whom occasionally, and as a great favor, he lends a little of his surplus profits to be applied to the making of new roads by means of which population may be more widely scattered, while he himself is thereby relieved from the danger of any increase in the competition for the *purchase* of wool, rags, or corn, or for the *sale* of cloth and iron, the commodities of which he is the owner.

The market whose prices for food regulate those of all the world is that of Great Britain. Whatever raises prices there raises those of New York and Boston, Chicago and St. Louis. How trivial was the quantity that in the first three years of the war was absorbed by that market, and how low were the prices obtained, have above been shown. Why were prices, at a time of real scarcity, so very low? Because we had so much to sell. Had only one-fourth of what we sent been retained at home for the consumption of men engaged in mining coal and ore and making iron, while another fourth had been retained for the supply of men, women, and children coming from abroad to work in our mines, our factories, and our fields, *we should have obtained almost as much for the remaining half as we did obtain for the whole.* That, however, is not all. Had we sent but one-half the quantity, and had the difference of price thus produced been but a single shilling sterling per bushel, that difference would have been felt by every bushel of the whole thousand millions produced in the loyal States, giving to be divided among their producers *an additional two hundred and fifty millions of dollars,* and enabling them to buy more cloth and more iron, and thus to live better, while so improving their machinery of production as to give them greatly more to sell in succeeding years. Had it made, *as it certainly would have done,* a difference of eighteen pence a bushel, the difference to our farmers—leaving altogether out of view corresponding differences in the prices of all their other products—would have been *little less than four hundred millions.* That amount, at the least, is it that they have paid in each of the last three years, for having, during a long period of years, so repeatedly crushed out the cotton and woollen manufactures, the coal, iron, and other important branches of industry; and in that way it has been that they have built up, at their own cost, "the large capitals" which have so systematically been used by our British *friends* as "the great instruments of warfare against the competing capital of other countries." They, themselves, make the whip whose lash they so severely feel. They, themselves, fashion the club by means of which they are struck down at the feet of their foreign masters. They, themselves, by tolerating among their Representatives a perpetual agitation of the British free trade question, are now paving the way for a return to a state of colonial subjection greater than has existed at any period since the peace of 1783.

For proof of this allow me now to request you to look at the consequences that must inevitably follow from the recent action of your House in regard to the paper manufacture. Under that action printing paper can no longer be made in this country, and we have now to choose between going abroad for $25,000,000 of paper, or dispensing with our usual supplies of journals and of books.

Under the action of the last session we shall, whenever the price of gold falls, be obliged to go abroad for, as I believe, the whole of the iron now produced, and the whole of the coal now employed in making iron. Taking these two items together, and placing them at a gold value of only $150,000,000, the question now arises as to how we are to pay for them? Seeking an answer to this question we are led naturally to look to the state, in regard to prices and demand, of the great regulating market of the world, and, fortunately, one of the New York journals of the day furnishes, in an extract from a Liverpool letter, all the information that we need, as follows:—

"The wheat market continues without a symptom of revival. If your supplies were to fall off Germany would at once begin to increase her consignments to us. *The possibility of a rally in our home prices is thus effectually prevented, and the year closes with the price of bread at a point lower than has been known within modern experience.*"

Germany and America thus contending for the supply of a diminutive market, prices are "lower than have been known within all modern experience," and the market presents no "symptom of revival." In this state of things it is, that we are arranging for drawing from Europe hundreds of millions of dollars worth of paper, coal, and iron, to be paid for by crowding on the British market all the flour and all the pork and beef now employed in fabricating the first, and in mining and converting the others! Such being the tendency of all our present legislation, am I, my dear sir, much in error in asserting that, often as our farmers have been "brayed" in the British free trade "mortar" their "foolishness" has not yet "departed from them?"

All that has thus far been done towards increasing our dependence on the diminutive British market constitutes, however, but one of the steps in that direction. The repeal of the paper duty has rendered necessary a movement towards the abolition of all duties affecting the materials required for the paper manufacture. Of these soda ash, of which our consumption is probably 40,000 tons, is one of the most important. Why have we not made it? Why do we not now make it? Why is it that the Iowa farmer has been using his corn as fuel when there were thousands and tens of thousands of European men who would gladly have come and eaten it while engaged in converting into soda ash the coal, the lime, and the salt that underlie so much of the land of the Mississippi Valley? Because the country gives to the capitalist no security that he shall not be crushed out of existence after having expended hundreds of thousands of dollars in the erection of works required for the conversion of raw materials into the commodity we so greatly need! In the absence of such security, and in the presence of agitation such as has now succeeded, so far as your House, my dear sir, is concerned, in crushing out one of the greatest and most fundamental of our industries, we shall be required to continue year after year to give to our masters, the "wealthy capitalists" of England, corn in its natural state at a few cents per bushel, buying it then back again in the form of bleaching powders at pence per pound—thus giving the skin for sixpence, and repurchasing the tail for a shilling.

It being required of us that we now abandon the protective system, and look once more to Europe for that great market which, as we were assured in 1847, was before this time to take from us "breadstuffs" to the annual amount of hundreds of millions, it may be well here to inquire what it is that that system has done for our farmers in the short period that has elapsed since the abdication of Southern masters gave to the North once more the power of self-protection.

The total export from the port of New York, exclusive of specie, in the week ending January 24, is given by the *Evening Post* at $6,333,663. Of this there appears to have been of breadstuffs and provisions going to those European markets from which we are likely henceforth to be obliged to draw our paper and our iron, as follows:—

Beef	500 tierces.
Flour	110 barrels.
Bacon	49,228 pounds.

In the same week the exports from Boston amounted to $481,447, in which were included 151 tubs of butter for Liverpool. Of an export, from those two ports, of nearly seven millions, the whole amount of breadstuffs and provisions for Europe did not exceed $30,000, or less than *one-half of one per cent.* How the remainder of the vast sum was made up will be seen on an examination of the following list of exports to the Argentine Republic, which presents a very fair specimen of the whole, as given in the *Shipping List:*—

Sewing Machines	cases	142	Drugs	pkgs.	185
Hoop Skirts		21	Glassware	cases	81
Furniture		280	Hardware	pkgs.	438
Clocks		182	Petroleum	galls.	3,158
Manufactured Tobacco	lbs.	17,975	Wax	bbls.	10
Oars	pcs.	500	Naval Stores	pkgs.	20
Oak		235	Hops	bales	38
Varnish	bbls.	26	Woodenware	pkgs.	126
Spirits Tar	galls.	50	Pepper	bags	496
Shoe Pegs	bbls.	55	Cloves	bales	100
Nails	kegs	306	Lumber	feet	470,896
Perfumery	cases	75			

These articles, my dear sir, are merely the food of the laborer in another and higher form; and thus it is that, to the weekly extent of millions of dollars, our farmers are enabled, by means of a diversified industry, to relieve themselves from the necessity for forcing their products on the already glutted market of England. The total export of breadstuffs to Great Britain and Ireland, in the last five months, as given in a table now before me, has been as follows:—

Flour	59,998 barrels.
Wheat	1,305,183 bushels.
Corn	56,933 bushels.

To the Continent there have gone 2,669 barrels of flour, and 68,521 bushels of wheat. Such is the great European market to which we are now advised to look for all our supplies of cloth, paper, and iron! Such is the market in whose favor we are now required to sacrifice coal and iron industries whose total products, in their various forms, now exceed four hundred millions of dollars, nearly the whole of which vast sum goes, directly or indirectly, to the men who are employed in clearing the land or cultivating it!

Why, however, is it that so little food can be spared for Europe? *Because the domestic market has already become so large that prices are above the exportation standard.* Let us go ahead in the direction in which for three years past we have been moving—let us give to the makers of paper and the smelters of iron ore that security without which they *dare not* enlarge their works or increase their number—and the day will not then be far distant when we shall be *importers* of wheat, instead of exporters of it, making a market for all the products of Canada and enabling our own farmers and landholders to become rich and independent, instead of being, as in all time past they have been, the mere *serfs* of those "wealthy capitalists" whose first wish is that food may become cheaper, and cloth and iron dearer.

Forty years since, General Jackson asked of his countrymen the important question, "*Where has the American farmer a market for his surplus products?*" In answer thereto he spoke as follows, and nothing more accurate was ever written :—

"Except for cotton, he has neither a foreign nor a home market. *Does not this clearly prove, when there is no market either at home or abroad, that there is too much labor employed in agriculture, and that the channels of labor should be multiplied?* Common sense points out at once the remedy. Draw from agriculture the superabundant labor, employ it in mechanism and manufactures, thereby creating a home market for your breadstuffs, and distributing labor to a most profitable account, and benefits to the country will result. TAKE FROM AGRICULTURE IN THE UNITED STATES SIX HUNDRED THOUSAND MEN, WOMEN, AND CHILDREN, AND YOU AT ONCE GIVE A HOME MARKET FOR MORE BREADSTUFFS THAN ALL EUROPE NOW FURNISHES US. In short, sir, we have been too long subject to the policy of the British merchants. It is time we should become a little more Americanized, and, instead of feeding the paupers and laborers of Europe, feed our own, or else in a short time, by continuing our present policy, we shall all be paupers ourselves."

France and England have pursued the policy here recommended, and they are now the greatest exporters of food in the world, the annual amount, with each, counting by hundreds of millions of dollars. They, however, combine hundred-weights of food with pounds of wool, silk, and cotton, and thus enable the former readily to make its way throughout the outside world. We are now, in proportion to our numbers and resources, the smallest food exporters of the world, because we insist on sending the raw materials of cloth to be combined together in other and wiser countries.

The policy recommended by General Jackson was that of the protective period from 1828 to 1834, at the close of which we paid off the last remnant of our national debt. It was that of the period from 1842 to 1847, which commenced with a scene of almost universal ruin, and closed with an exhibit of prosperity such as the world had never before seen. It is the policy by means of which our farmers are now relieved from all necessity for forcing their products on foreign markets, to be there taken, at prices to be fixed by themselves, by "wealthy capitalists," who pay for them in cloth and iron, at prices also fixed by themselves.

For a portion of this relief they have been indebted to the demand created by large bodies of men employed in carrying muskets, but this is so far from being opposed to the view above presented that it furnishes proof conclusive of its truth. Change those men into miners and puddlers, producers of silks and cottons, watches and locomotives, and their demands for the various products of the earth will be greater than now they are. As it is, the farmer profits only by an increase in the prices of what he has to sell. As it then would be, he would add thereto a decrease of price in regard to all that he required to purchase. The truth of the Jacksonian doctrine is, thus, thoroughly demonstrated by the facts now presented in the consumption of our fleets and armies. As human pursuits become diversified land acquires value and the farmer becomes rich and independent.

Who, now, are the men who have combined together for the destruction of the great paper, coal, and iron industries, and for the reduction of the farmer to his former dependence on British markets? Let us see. They are—

I. Railroad owners, who, in the last three years, have taxed the farmer to the utmost of their ability by increasing the charge for transportation:

II. British agents who look to reduction in the price of food and augmentation in the price of iron for increase of their commissions:

III. Secessionists at home and abroad, in and out of Congress—men who look to bankruptcy of the National Treasury as the most certain means of obtaining elevation for themselves.

Against these should now be banded together—

I. Every farmer who desires to see the tax of transportation diminished and the value of his land increased:

II. Every laborer who desires to find himself in the condition of one of the owners of the land:

III. Every landholder who sees in liberal reward of labor a stimulus to that immigration by means of which the number of purchasers of land must be increased:

IV. Every man who sees that land increases rapidly in value as industry becomes more and more diversified, while declining as rapidly when furnaces and mills are closed and diversification dies away:

V. Every holder of a Government note, or bond, who sees that it is the Internal Revenue alone to which he and others like himself must in future look for payment of their interest:

VI. Every lover of his country who sees that with every increase in the domestic commerce there is an increase in the number of the threads by means of which the Union is to be held together:

VII. Every man who appreciates the fact that it is to that British free trade by means of which we have been compelled to look to a distant market as the one in which to make all our exchanges, that we have been indebted for the loss of property and of life that has resulted from the great rebellion; and,

VIII. Every man who feels as an American should feel in reference to the conduct, throughout the past four years, of that British people which teaches everywhere "free trade" as the most efficient means of securing a monopoly of the machinery of transportation and conversion for the world at large.

If this nation is ever to become really independent; if it is ever to become *Americanized;* if it is ever to occupy that position in the world to which the vast amount of mineral wealth placed at its command so well entitles it; if it is ever to cease to be a mere puppet in the hands of foreign agents; if it is ever to be placed in a position to perform the duties of its great mission to the poor and oppressed throughout the earth; its people must learn that in the real and permanent interests of all the portions of society there is a perfect harmony, and that of all who should desire the establishment of that certain protection which shall authorize the capitalist to open mines, build furnaces, improve water-powers, and erect mills, there are none whose interests look so much in that direction as do those of the landowner and the farmer. All, however, are greatly interested; all should learn to appreciate the advantages that must result from combination for relief from that foreign domination under which we have so long and so severely suffered; and all should study the admirable lesson taught in the following fable by our old friend Æsop:—

"An old man had many sons, who were often falling out with one another. When the father had exerted his authority, and used other means in order to reconcile them, and all to no purpose, at last he had recourse to this expedient: he ordered his sons to be called before him, and a short bundle of sticks to be brought; and then commanded them, one by one, to try if, with all their might and strength, they could any of them break it. They all tried, but to no purpose; for the sticks being closely and compactly bound up together, it was impossible for the force of man to do it. After this, the father ordered the bundle to be untied, and gave a single stick to each of his sons, at the same time bidding him try to break it; which, when each did with all imaginable ease, the father addressed himself to them to this effect: 'O my sons, behold the power of unity! for if you, in like manner, would but keep yourselves strictly conjoined in the bonds of friendship, it would not be in the power of any mortal to hurt you; but when once the ties of brotherly affection are dissolved, how soon do you fall to pieces, and are liable to be violated by every injurious hand that assaults you!' "

The men of the North have shown their appreciation of this lesson by the determination they have manifested to maintain the Union of the States. Let the people of all those States show their appreciation of it by combining together for securing permanently to the farmer such a market for his products as shall free him wholly from the tyranny of the "wealthy capitalists" abroad; let them determine that American food *shall* go to the production of all the cloth, all the paper, and all the iron they need to use, and we shall then have discovered the true and certain mode of *outdoing England without fighting her.*

In another letter I propose to examine the railroad question, remaining meanwhile, with great regard and respect,

Yours, very truly,

HENRY C. CAREY.

Hon. Schuyler Colfax.

Philadelphia, Jan. 30, 1865.

THE RAILROAD QUESTION.

LETTER ELEVENTH.

DEAR SIR:—

THE man who habitually retains himself in a position to be obliged to seek for purchasers of his labor or its products rarely fails to reap ruin as its result. He who, on the contrary, so places himself as to be enabled to compel purchasers to come to him, finds his power of accumulation increase with each succeeding year, and ends with colossal fortune. The first is that one in which the American people, guided by British agents, have always kept themselves, and we have the result in a war that must have brought universal ruin had it not brought with it also emancipation from that British free trade policy whose effects are so well described by General Jackson in the admirable letter already given. The second is that in which the people of France, under a system of protection maintained with a persistence that has no parallel in history, have placed themselves. The whole world is compelled to go to them to buy, and *they* fix the prices at which they choose to sell. The world is compelled to go there to sell, and *they* are thus enabled to fix the prices at which they choose to purchase. The result exhibits itself in a most extraordinary increase in the value of lands and houses, the figures of which I have seen but cannot at the moment find. Well, however, do I recollect that they were of a character calculated to excite astonishment even in one who had witnessed the effect on western lands of a steady flow of emigration from the East.

The first has been governed by that class of men of which Mr. Secretary Walker is the type; that class which proclaims that this is naturally "an agricultural country," and that we must seek abroad a market for our "breadstuffs and provisions"—thereby so limiting our people in their modes of employment as to make the country little more than a mere puppet in the hands of foreign traders. The other has been, in this respect at least, governed by men of whom the great Colbert is the type—men who have clearly seen that national independence was to be achieved by means of bringing the consumer to take his place by the side of the producer, and thereby giving value to both land and labor. The results exhibit themselves in the fact that France now controls the movements of all Europe, while the people of this country, with natural advantages a thousandfold greater, and almost as large a population, now find themselves compelled to abandon the Monroe doctrine and fight for national existence—France, meanwhile, obtaining command of our immediate neighbor, Mexico.

Shall we ever do better? It may well be doubted. Often as our farmers, our merchants, and our transporters have been "brayed" in the British free trade "mortar," their "foolishness" has not yet "departed from them;" and, judging from recent proceedings in Congress, it would seem that, sad as has been our experience, they are little likely even now to profit by it. Nothing, as it would seem, can open their eyes to a perception of the great fact, that in the real and permanent interests of the West and the East, the North and the South, as well as in those of the ship-owner, the railroad proprietor, the miner, the iron-master, the land-owner, and the laborer, there is a perfect harmony, and that it is absolutely impossible to injure any one of them without at the same time injuriously affecting all the rest. Blind to this are they all, and, as a consequence of this it is, that we find western land-holders and laborers combining with railroad managers for promoting the adoption of a policy that each and every one of them would bitterly denounce could he but be persuaded to pause a little in his course and study carefully what had been the effect in the past of measures similar to those whose adoption he now so earnestly advocates.

Of all, there are none who have shown themselves so blind to their true interests as those same railroad managers. All experience teaches that roads are profitable in the ratio borne by way to through business, and unprofitable in the ratio borne by through to way business. Why is it so? Because with the growth of this latter they become independent; whereas, with increase in the proportion borne by through business they become more and more dependent. In proof of this we may take the fact, that such has been the competition for this latter that produce has, on many occasions, been forwarded from Chicago to New York more cheaply than from Buffalo, and more cheaply from this latter than from either Rochester or Syracuse. In this manner they first offer bounties on emigration from the older States, and then find themselves compelled to enlarge their capital and extend their roads with a view to retain their business. Common sense might, as one would think, teach them that by aiding in the development of our great mineral resources they would be creating a local traffic that could be carried on at small cost and with great profit to themselves; yet have they invariably been found combining with British agents in opposition to such development, thereby imposing upon themselves a necessity for still further extension of their lines, with steady diminution in their power to pay their stockholders.

Our railroad history covers a period of only five and thirty years, and it may now be not unprofitable to cast our eyes back over that period with a view to ascertain what are the lessons for the future that may be thence deduced.

In 1832, the railroad interest insisted upon depriving our furnaces of the manufacture of railroad bars. In the ten succeeding years many roads were made, and all with British bars bought at the highest prices. As a consequence the cost of roads was great, and at the close of the free trade period in 1842 the railroad interest was in a state of almost universal ruin. Why was it so? Because the road-makers had united with British traders in urging upon the country a policy whose effect had been that of making them yearly more and more dependent upon a through trade that could not be made to yield a profit. The domestic market for food had been greatly lessened, while that of Europe had failed to grow.

The tariff of 1842 imposed a heavy duty on railroad bars, and then for the first time was their manufacture commenced on this side of the Atlantic. Iron generally being well protected the production rose in half a dozen years to 800,000 tons, and the consumption to 900,000. Labor being everywhere in demand, immigration trebled in that brief period. Towns and villages increased in number and in size. The local traffic therefore grew, and railroads became once more profitable to their proprietors.

Taking no lesson from experience railroad and canal owners united in beating down protection, and giving us Mr. Walker's free trade tariff of 1846. How they profited of this may be judged from the following figures giving the receipts of some of the principal works in the period from 1842 to 1849:—

	New York canals.	Balt. and Ohio railroad.	Pennsylvania canals.	Total.
1842,	1,749,000	426,000	903,000	3,078,000
1844,	2,446,000	658,000	1,164,000	4,268,000
1846,	2,756,000	881,000	1,357,000	4,994,000
1847,	3,635,000	1,101,000	1,587,000	6,323,000
1848,	3,252,000	1,231,000	1,550,000	6,033,000
1849,	3,266,000	1,241,000	1,580,000	6,087,000

Under protection the receipts more than doubled, as here is shown. As the British free trade system became more fully operative they declined, thus presenting a striking commentary on Mr. Walker's assertion, made but two years previously, that under a free trade system "our own country, with its pre-eminent advantages, would measure its annual trade in imports and exports by thousands of millions of dollars."

At that moment, however, California had already begun to furnish to the world its golden treasures, thus making a market for labor under which immigration for several years rapidly increased. That period, however, terminated with 1854, and thenceforward railroad property, *as a natural consequence of continued railroad agitation for the abolition of the duty on railroad iron*, rapidly decreased in value, as is shown by the following figures :—

	1852–3.	1855.
Baltimore and Ohio	98	56
Boston and Worcester	105	87½
New York and Erie	85	52
Cleveland and Pittsburg	93	70
Michigan Southern	118	97
Cincinnati and Dayton	102	85
Pennsylvania Central	93	88
Camden and Amboy	149	128
Boston and Maine	102	94

From that date to the opening of the rebellion immigration declined; internal development almost ceased; and railroad property so much depreciated that the average value of the New York Central, Erie, Hudson River, Reading, Michigan Central, Michigan Southern, Rhode Island, Cleveland and Toledo, Illinois Central, and Galena and Ohio roads was *only forty-two per cent.*

The war came, bringing with it protection to the farmer, accompanied by an increase in the value of railroad property, as exhibited in the following figures giving the average prices of the several roads last above referred to :—

January, 1855	1860	1862	1863	1864
42	56	51	95	143

Seeking now the cause of the vast change that is here exhibited we find it in the following passages from Reports just made by two important Western roads—the Southern Michigan and the Cleveland and Pittsburg Railroad.

From the first we learn that—

"Although the decline on the through business is at the rate of $30,000 to $40,000 per month, so great has been the increase in local traffic that the aggregate earnings for January, 1865, show an increase of about $50,000 over the corresponding month last year. Although there has been no diminution in the number of employees, the aggregate number of miles run by passenger trains is now 5000 per week less than it was before the issuing of the passport order. There is, therefore, a considerable saving in running expenses."

And from the second that—

"The great increase of freight upon the road has come in a very important degree from two articles of traffic which may be considered the staple of your road, naturally and legitimately belonging to it. These articles are coal and iron ore of Lake Superior. The coal interest was one of the principal agencies in planning and building this road, and those early projectors of the enterprise have always looked to the development of the coal mines on the line of the road as a sure and steady means of remuneration. The coal trade has from the first held an important place among the various sources of revenue to your road. It has steadily increased with the progress of years, and as manufacturing has been more extensively undertaken, and as new demands for coal from regions before unsupplied have arisen, the transportation over your road has been greatly increased in amount."

What is true of these two roads, is almost equally so of those of the country at large, the existing prosperity of the whole railroad interest having come as a natural consequence of great developments of mineral wealth. Take, for instance, petroleum, of which to the extent of $46,000,000 was sent to market in the past year, and see, my dear sir, how large have already become its contributions to railroad revenues. Look further, however, and see how enormous they must become when Ohio, Virginia, and other States shall have sunk their wells and erected their engines, and when refineries shall, at the place of production, fit it for cheap transportation to the remotest corners of Maine in the Northeast and Texas in the Southwest, Florida in the Southeast and Nevada in the Northwest;

and then endeavor to satisfy yourself to what extent it is that every road in the country is interested in the successful prosecution of the great work of development that has but now commenced. Take next the 13,000,000 tons of coal now mined, and follow them in their travels throughout the Union, paying toll directly to roads in the East and roads in the West, and indirectly to every one in the whole extent of the loyal States. Add now to them the 1,300,000 tons of pig metal at present made, and follow them, in all their various forms of railroad bars, stoves, pipes, knives, and engines, and then determine to what extent they have contributed to give to the roads of the country their present value.

Study next, I pray you, the perfect harmony of all these various interests, and satisfy yourself how shortsighted are the men who believe in national discords. What is it that has so suddenly given an almost fabulous value to the great oil region of the West? Is it not the almost immediate presence of the great machine-shops of Ohio, Indiana, Illinois, and Pennsylvania? What would be its value were its owners obliged to seek in Birmingham for engines? It would have none whatsoever. To whom, however, are we indebted for those shops? Is it not to men who have sunk mines and built furnaces, others who have mined coal and ore, and still others who have converted raw material into pigs and pipes? That it is so, cannot be questioned. The harmony of all those interests is absolute and complete.

Equally so is that which exists between the men who make and those who need to purchase the railroad bar. Many millions of dollars worth of oil go to market, there to be exchanged for sugar and coffee, cloth, iron, and the thousand other commodities needed for a population that is increasing in wealth and numbers, and at every stage of their progress they contribute towards railroad dividends. So, too, with the iron and the coal. I have now before me the accounts of a single iron establishment that paid last year, in railroad tolls, no less a sum than $200,000. Judging from this, at how many millions might we safely fix the contributions of coal and iron to the maintenance of the railroad interest?

To enable us to form an accurate judgment of the amount of such contributions by the great fundamental industries, let us for a moment look to the effect that would at once result from their annihilation. Would it not certainly diminish by two-thirds the real value of every railroad in the Union? That it would do so, cannot be questioned. What, then, would be the effect were we in the next seven years to double, even if we should not treble, the product of our mines, our furnaces, our rolling-mills, and our wells? Could it fail to be that of giving to all railroad property a fixed and certain value, even when estimated in gold, greater than it ever yet has known? That it could not fail to do so, is absolutely certain. That you may now be led, my dear sir, to arrive, in this respect, at the same belief with myself, I would ask you to look to the fact that a coal mine is a vast magazine of *power;* that thousands of tons of coal can be made to do the work of hundreds of thousands of men; that in the extent and variety of metallic deposits we are ahead of the whole of Europe combined; that POWER ALONE is needed for bringing to light the vast treasures of the iron mountains of Missouri on the west, and of the Adirondack on the east—of the great iron and copper beds of the shores of Lake Superior—of the wealth-abounding hills of Tennessee—of the great lead deposits of Illinois and Iowa—of the coal, iron, and gold abounding districts of Virginia—of the zinc and iron deposits of New Jersey—and of the granite hills of New England; that the power at our command is equal to that of almost the whole earth combined; that that now used in Great Britain alone is estimated as being equal to the labor of 600,000,000 of men; that by a proper application of our energies we might within the next decade go far beyond even that vast amount; that production increases almost geometrically as the power applied increases arithmetically; that exchanges increase with the increase of production; that the power to contribute to the maintenance of roads increases with a rapidity far exceeding that of production; and then determine for yourself how magnificent is the future that will open itself to the eye of every railroad manager when he and his fellow-proprietors shall have arrived at the conclusion, that there is a perfect harmony in the interests of the men who make iron and those who need to use it, and that an enlightened self-interest demands of them that they shall ask of Congress the establishment of such a revenue system as shall give to the capitalist that certainty in regard to the future which is needed for enabling us, before the lapse of another decade, to place ourselves side by side with Great Britain in the production of many of the most important metals, and before the close of another to leave her far behind, thus giving to the farmer a market near at hand for all his products.

The mind is lost in contemplation of the marvellous amount of wealth and power that has by a beneficent Creator been placed at our command. Still more, however, is it lost in wonder when studying the slow degrees by which we have arrived at the idea that prosperity among our people, freedom to the slave, and power and influence among the nations of the world, were to come to us only as a consequence of the application of that vast power to the development of that wonderful wealth. More than thirty years since, at the close of the protective period which began in 1828, our consumption of iron was 300,000 tons. Ten years later, at the close of a long and dreary free-trade period, with a population one-third greater, the consumption was still but little more. Five years later, at the close of the protective period of 1842, our production had already trebled, and so great had become the demand, that the import of foreign iron was nearly as great as it had been in 1842. Ten years still later, with a population again a third increased, and with all the advantage of California gold developments, our production, under the British free-trade system, had diminished, while our total consumption had scarcely at all increased. Of the four years that have since passed by, one was a period of universal prostration, and yet, in the three that have succeeded our consumption has been carried up to a point nearly one-third higher than that at which it stood at the outbreak of the great rebellion. These are remarkable facts, and with them is connected another series of phenomena of the highest importance to railroad proprietors, which, however, seems to have escaped their notice. *Whenever the domestic production of iron has been advancing railroad property has paid good dividends, while dividends have always declined as furnaces and rolling-mills became idle and their proprietors became bankrupt.* In 1832, the first of the protective periods above referred to, railroads had scarcely yet made their appearance on the stage, but transporters of every description were highly prosperous. In 1842, at the close of the first of the above-named free-trade periods, furnaces were closed and railroad companies were bankrupt. In 1847, the second protective period, ironmasters were prosperous and railroad companies paid good dividends. In 1854, under a temporary California excitement, railroad stocks were high and ironmasters were building rolling-mills. In 1860, at the close of the last free-trade period, railroad stocks were selling, as has been already shown, at an average of 42 per cent., and mills, mines, and furnaces were everywhere closed. To-day, after three years of protection, all is changed, *ironmasters having doubled their production and thus enabled railroad stocks to go again to par.*

The direct connection between the road and iron interests is here so clearly obvious that it is almost marvellous that the former should so long have failed to see it. More wonderful is it, however, that seeing what has but now occurred, they should yet continue so blind to their true interests as to array themselves in opposition to any measure on the part of Congress that shall tend to give that security for the future without which the capitalist *will not* give his time and his means to the opening of mines, or to the building of furnaces and mills. To induce him so to apply his powers he *must* have protection against that system so well described in an extract from a Parliamentary Report to which your attention has already more than once been called, and which, as I have said, should be read day by day, week by week, month by month, and year by year, by every man who desires to see the Union maintained, with constant increase in the power of the nation to command the respect of the other communities of the earth. It is as follows:—

"The laboring classes generally, in the manufacturing districts of this country and especially in the iron and coal districts, are very little aware of the extent to which they are often indebted for their being employed at all to the immense *losses* which their employers voluntarily incur in bad times, in order *to destroy foreign competition, and to gain and keep possession of foreign markets.* Authentic instances are well known of employers having in such times carried on their works at a loss amounting in the aggregate to three or four hundred thousand pounds in the course of three or four years. If the efforts of those who encourage the combinations to restrict the amount of labor and to produce strikes were to be successful for any length of time, the great accumulations of capital could no longer be made *which enable a few of the most wealthy capitalists to overwhelm all foreign competition in times of great depression*, and thus to clear the way for the *whole trade* to step in when prices revive, and to carry on a great business before *foreign* capital can again accumulate to such an extent as to be able to establish a competition in prices with any chance of success. *The large capitalists of this country are the great instruments of warfare against the competing capital of foreign countries*, and are *the most essential* instruments now remaining by which our manufacturing supremacy can be maintained; the other elements—cheap labor, abundance of raw material, means of communication, and skilled labor—being rapidly in process of being equalized."

The wealthy British "capitalists" here described have their agents everywhere, and everywhere prepared for combination with every little private or local interest for the removal of grievances of which *they know their masters and themselves to be the cause.* What *they* desire, as they know full well, is that food may be cheap and iron high in price. What *we* desire, and what by means of protection we are seeking to obtain, is that the farmer may from year to year be enabled to obtain more spades and ploughs, and better means of transportation, in exchange for less and less of food. When, however, the farmer complains of the low price of corn, he finds the agent always at hand, Mephistophiles-like, to whisper in his ear that but for protection spades and ploughs would be cheaper, while food would command a higher price. When the railroad manager seeks to buy iron, he points to the low price at which British iron might be purchased, wholly omitting to call the attention of his hearer to the facts, that *British iron is always cheap when American people build furnaces, and when American railroad companies make good dividends, and always dear when American furnaces have been blotted out of existence, when their owners have been made bankrupt, and when American railroad stocks are of little worth.* In proof of this, I now give you the following facts as they present themselves in the Reports on Commerce and Navigation for the several years above referred to:—

At the close of the protective period which commenced in 1828 and terminated in 1833—that one in which for the first time the iron manufacture made a great forward movement, and therefore the most prosperous one that the country had ever known, the price at which British bar iron, rails included, was shipped to this country, was *forty dollars.*

Eight years later, in 1841, when our mechanics were seeking alms—when our farmers could find no market—when furnaces and mills were everywhere closed, and their owners everywhere ruined—when States were repudiating, and the National Treasury was wholly unable to meet its small engagements—the shipping price of British bars had been advanced to *fifty dollars.*

Eight years later, in 1849, after protection had carried up our domestic product to 800,000 tons, and after the British free trade tariff of 1846 had once again placed our ironmasters under the heel of the "wealthy English capitalist," we find the latter energetically using that potent "instrument of warfare" by means of which he "gains and keeps possession of foreign markets," and supplying bar iron at THIRTY DOLLARS per ton. In what manner, however, was the railroad interest paying for a reduction like this, by means of which they were being enabled to save on their repairs a tenth or a twentieth of one per cent. on their respective capitals? Seeking an answer to this question I find in the *Merchant's Magazine* a comparison of the prices in February, 1848 and 1850, of thirteen important roads, by which it is shown that in that short period there had been a decline of *more than thirty per cent.!* This would seem to be paying somewhat dearly for the whistle of cheap iron; and yet it is but trifling as compared with information contained in a paragraph which follows in which are given the names of numerous important roads, whose cost had been very many millions of dollars, but which "from prices quoted, and those merely nominal, seem to be of little or no value—not enough, nor one-fourth enough, to pay interest on the sums advanced for their creation."

At the close of another term of similar length, say in 1857, we arrive at a scene of ruin more general than any that had been witnessed since the closing years of that British free trade period which terminated with the universal crash of '42. How very low were then railroad stocks has been already shown. What, however, was the price at which British ironmasters were willing, now that they had so effectually crushed out competition, to meet the demands of railroad managers? Were they still willing to accept $30 per ton as the shipping price? Did they *then* manifest any desire to help the friends who had so largely aided them in "gaining and keeping possession" of this American market? Far from it! The more that railroad stocks went down, as a consequence of failure of the domestic commerce, the more determined did the British masters of our American stockholders show themselves, Shylock-like, determined to exact "the pound of flesh." In this unhappy period the shipping price of bars was $48, and that of railroad iron $42, the average having been FORTY-FOUR DOLLARS, or nearly fifty per cent. advance on the prices accepted in 1849, when our foreign lords and masters had been engaged in "*overwhelming all foreign competition in times of great depression*," and thus "*clearing the way for the whole trade to step in when prices revived, and to carry on a great business before foreign capital could again accu-*

mulate so as to be able to establish a competition in prices with any chance of success."

Twice thus, at intervals of eight years each, have we had low British prices and great American prosperity as a consequence of the adoption of a policy under which American competition for the *sale* of iron has largely grown. Twice, at similar intervals, have we had high British prices and universal American depression as a consequence of the re-adoption of that system under which we have been compelled to compete in a foreign market for the *purchase* of British iron. Twice, thus, have American railroad managers been "brayed" in the British free trade "mortar," and twice have American transporters found prosperity by aid of those protective measures to which they have always shown themselves so much opposed. Their British free trade experience had been a somewhat sad one. Have they profited of it? Let us see.

Another eight year period has now passed by, and we reach the present year 1865, *with railroad stocks selling for a thousand millions of dollars that would not, at its commencement, have sold for five hundred millions.* What has caused this wonderful change? The re-creation, by means of a protective tariff, of a great internal commerce, *and nothing else.* Under that tariff mines have been opened, mills and furnaces have been built, demand has been created for labor and labor's products, commerce has grown, and road proprietors have participated with farmers in the advantages resulting from the creation of a great domestic market which are so well described in an extract from the recent message of Governor Yates, of Illinois, already given, but here reproduced because of its important bearing on the question now before us:—

"As a State, notwithstanding the war, we have prospered beyond all former precedents. Notwithstanding nearly two hundred thousand of the most athletic and vigorous of our population have been withdrawn from the field of production, the area of land now under cultivation is greater than at any former period, and the census of 1865 will exhibit an astonishing increase in every department of material industry and advancement; in a great increase of agricultural, manufacturing, and mechanical wealth; in new and improved modes for production of every kind; in the substitution of machinery for the manual labor withdrawn by the war; in the triumphs of invention; in the wonderful increase of railroad enterprise; in the universal activity of business, in all its branches; in the rapid growth of our cities and villages; in the bountiful harvests, and in an unexampled material prosperity, prevailing on every hand; while, at the same time, the educational institutions of the people have in no way declined. Our colleges and schools, of every class and grade, are in the most flourishing condition; our benevolent institutions, State and private, are kept up and maintained; and, in a word, our prosperity is as complete and ample as though no tread of armies or beat of drum had been heard in all our borders."

The picture here given is that of every loyal State of the Union, and yet it is but the beginning of the change that is to be accomplished by means of the establishment of perfect commercial independence. Railroad proprietors have already profited of it to the extent of hundreds of millions of dollars, and they have yet to profit to the extent of many other hundreds of millions by the further opening of mines, the further building of mills, and the further development of the wonderful amount of mineral wealth placed by a kind Providence at our command, and waiting only the application of that power which now lies hidden beneath the soil of so many thousands of square miles of all these central States. So having profited in the past, and having in view so large a profit in the future, it might be supposed that they would now, at least, be content. Are they so? Are they disposed to let well alone! Has their "foolishness" at length departed from them? Having been now so repeatedly "brayed" in the free trade "mortar," are they now at last awakened to a sense of the advantages that must inevitably result to themselves from carrying up our production of iron from hundreds of thousands to millions of tons? Do they see that, to enable the Union to hold together, we must establish such an internal commerce as will permit of exchanges being made between its various parts freed from the intervention of British agents, British ships, and British ports? *Are their eyes yet open to a perception of the fact that the country that makes the most iron is the one into whose hands must fall the direction of the commerce of the world?* Have they, in any manner, profited by the sad experience of the past? To all these questions the reply must, unhappily, be a negative one. Like the Bourbons, they have learned nothing, and have forgotten none of their free trade prejudices, and it is much to be feared they never will, or can, do so. Despite all the lessons of the past they have now allied themselves with British agents for crushing out those great fundamental industries to which alone we can look for that success in the war in which we are now engaged without which railroad stocks and bonds, Government bonds, and property of all descriptions must lose two-thirds of their present value.

The men most active in the work of destruction are, strangely enough, precisely those whose real and permanent interests should lead them in the opposite direction—the representatives of trans-Mississippi roads. Of all our people they are those who should most desire to promote immigration, and yet they close their eyes to the fact that immigration grows with development of our mineral resources and declines as furnaces are blown out and rolling mills are closed. Of all, they should most desire that existing railroad property should be productive, yet do they close their eyes to the fact that such property has always declined in value as furnaces and mills were closed, and grown again as mills were once again opened, and as furnaces were built. Of all, they should most desire that a low price of foreign iron should operate as a check upon our iron-masters, yet do they close their eyes to the fact that such iron has always fallen in price as domestic competition has grown, and risen again as soon as they and others like them had succeeded in enabling the "wealthy English capitalists" to destroy that competition. Of all, they are those who have suffered most and learned the least.

It was under the protective tariff of 1828 that immigration first became a matter of much importance. Furnaces were then built, internal commerce grew rapidly, farmers became rich, transporters were well rewarded for their services, immigration trebled in its amount, and American competition compelled the British iron-masters to furnish iron at a moderate price.

Eight years later all this was changed, the American makers of roads and of iron being both together ruined, labor being everywhere in excess of the demand, and immigration remaining stationary at a point but little higher than it had so promptly reached in 1834.

Eight years still later we find that under protection the production of iron had trebled, thereby making such demand for labor as to have carried the number of immigrants up to little short of 300,000.

At the close of another period of similar length, passed under the free trade system, we find labor to have been in excess of demand while railroad owners were being ruined, and immigration to have so far declined as to have ceased to merit much consideration.

Again, in 1865, we have reached a period of some protection to the greatest of all the industries of the world. Labor is, therefore, in demand. Immigration grows, and with it the value of railroad stock, while British iron is very cheap.

The close connection that here is shown to exist between immigration and protection, as well as between prosperity and a low price of British iron, ought surely to be sufficient to satisfy our trans-Mississippi friends of the absolute necessity that exists for giving to the great departments of industry that certain protection which is required for securing a rapid increase in the domestic competition for supplying the market with coal, paper, leather, and iron of all descriptions. They have land in abundance, and their mineral wealth is great beyond all calculation. What they need is *power.* To obtain that they must have men to mine their coal and their ore, to build engines, to clear their lands, and to make their roads. Men come *always* when we have protection. They fly from us *always* when we are subjected to the British free trade system. Can they not, then, see that all their real and permanent interests are in perfect harmony with those of the older States? Must they be once more "brayed" in the free trade "mortar" before they will come to understand these things?

So much for the past, and now, for a moment, let us look to the future. To all appearances it will be needed, within a very brief period, to relay all the southern roads, and there will be need for hundreds of thousands of tons of rails. Are we preparing for this? Are we now building furnaces and rolling mills? We are not! On the contrary, they are being closed, even the present taxes, as compared with the duties on that made abroad, being so oppressive that the work of manufacture can no longer be carried on with any profit. It is seen, too, that the nearer we approach a gold value the heavier become the internal taxes, and the more does the foreign manufacturer tend to become *protected against the domestic one.* Let this continue but a little longer, and let occasion arise for laying those Southern roads, and what then will be the price of British iron? Cannot our railroad managers see that, in pursuing their present course, they are not only "killing the goose that lays the golden egg," but also providing for subjecting themselves to a taxation for the benefit of our British *friends* that, combined with the loss of the domestic traffic, must cause the price of their stock to fall again to the low price at which it stood in 1857? Cannot they see that now, as always heretofore, they are playing cards that have been placed in their hands by men whose one great object in life is that of having food and labor cheap while iron is maintained at the highest price? Can they not see that the objects they should always have in view are directly the reverse of this, their prosperity coming always with rise in the profits of the farmer and in the wages of the laborer, and decline in the price of iron? They are now laboring to arrest the growing tendency to emigration from the shores of Europe; and yet, every man who can be attracted here becomes, from the moment of his arrival, a contributor to their revenues, while preparing, by means of procreation, for a further increase in the number of such contributors, and in the powers of each and all.

It is surely time that our railroad managers should awaken to the fact that their interests are so perfectly in harmony with those of the men who mine coal and make iron that every blow levelled at the latter tells directly upon themselves. When they shall do so—when they shall have arrived at the conclusion that these two great interests should stand shoulder to shoulder with each other, and that an enlightened self-interest ought to prompt them to aid in securing the adoption of measures looking to the incorporation of home-grown food in every yard of cloth, every ream of paper, and every hide of leather consumed on this side of the Atlantic—we shall then at length be fairly on the road toward finding how it is that we may *outdo England without fighting her.*

Sincerely hoping that the day may not be far distant when all this shall be done, and when our people shall, to use the words of Jackson, become a little more *Americanized*, I remain, my dear sir, with great regard and respect,

Yours very truly,

HENRY C. CAREY.

Hon. Schuyler Colfax.

Philadelphia, February 10, 1865.

THE CURRENCY QUESTION.

LETTER TWELFTH.

DEAR SIR:—

Side by side with the question of protection, and equal with it in its importance, stands that of the Currency, to which I propose now to ask your attention.

Had it been possible, on the 4th of March, 1861, to take a bird's-eye view of the whole Union, the phenomena presenting themselves for examination would have been as follows:—

Millions of men and women would have been seen who were wholly or partially unemployed, because of inability to find persons able and willing to pay for service.

Hundreds of thousands of workmen, farmers, and shopkeepers would have been seen holding articles of various kinds for which no purchasers could be found.

Tens of thousands of country traders would have been seen poring over their books seeking, but vainly seeking, to discover in what direction they might look for obtaining the means with which to discharge their city debts.

Thousands of city traders would have been seen endeavoring to discover how they might obtain the means with which to pay their notes.

Thousands of mills, factories, furnaces, and workshops large and small, would have been seen standing idle while surrounded by persons who desired to be employed; and

Tens of thousands of bank, factory, and railroad proprietors would have been seen despairing of obtaining dividends by means of which they might be enabled to go to market.

High above all these would have been seen a National Treasury wholly empty, and to all appearance little likely ever again to be filled.

Why was all this? The laborer needing food, and the farmer clothing, why did they not exchange? Because of the absence of power on the part of the former to give to the latter anything with which he could purchase either hats or coats.

The village shopkeeper desired to pay his city debts. Why did he not? because the neighboring mill was standing idle while men and women, indebted to him, were wholly unemployed.

The city trader could not meet his notes, because his village correspondents could not comply with their engagements. The doctor could not collect his bills. The landlord could not collect his rents; and all, from laborer to landlord, found themselves compelled to refrain from the purchase of those commodities to whose consumption the National Treasury had been used to look for the supplies upon which it thus far had depended.

With all, the difficulty resulted from the one great fact already indicated in regard to the laborer. If *he* could have found any one willing to give him something that the farmer would accept from him in exchange for food—that the farmer could then pass to his neighbor shopkeeper in exchange for cloth—that that neighbor could then pass to the city trader in satisfaction of his debt—and that this latter could then pass to the bank, to his counsel, his physician, or his landlord—the *societary circulation* would at once have been re-established and the public health restored.

That one thing, however, was scarcely anywhere to be found. Its generic name was *money*, but the various species were known as gold, silver, copper, and circulating notes. Some few persons possessed them in larger or smaller quantities; but, the total amount being very small when compared with that which was required, their owners would not part with the use of them except on terms so onerous as to be ruinous to the borrowers. As a consequence of this, the city trader paid ten, twelve, and fifteen per cent. per annum for the use of what he needed, charging twice that, to the village shopkeeper, in the prices of his goods. The latter, of course, found it necessary to do the same by his neighbors, charging nearly cent. per cent.; and thus was the whole burthen resulting from deficiency in the supply of a medium of exchange thrown upon the class which least could bear it, the working people of the country—farmers, mechanics, and laborers. As a consequence of this they shrunk in their proportions as the societary circulation became more and more impeded, while with those who held in their hands the regulation of the money supply the effect exhibited itself in the erection of those great palaces which now stand almost side by side with tenement houses whose occupants, men, women, and children, count by hundreds. The rich thus grew richer as the poor grew poorer.

Why was all this? Why did they not use the gold of which California had already sent us so many hundreds of millions? Because we had most carefully followed in the train of British free trade teachers who had assured our people that the safe, true, and certain road towards wealth and power was to be found in the direction of sending wheat, flour, corn, pork, and wool to England in their rudest form, and then buying them back again, at quadruple prices, paying the difference in the products of Californian mines! Because we had in this manner, for a long period of years, been selling whole skins for sixpence and buying back tails for a shilling! Because we had thus compelled our people to remain idle while consuming food and clothing, the gold meanwhile being sent to purchase other food and clothing for the workmen of London and Paris, Lyons, Manchester, and Birmingham!

Why, however, when circulating notes could so easily be made, did not the banks supply them, when all around them would so gladly have allowed interest for their use? Because those notes were redeemable in a commodity of which, although California gave us much, we could no longer retain even the slightest portion, the quantity required abroad for payment of heavy interest, and for the purchase of foreign food in the forms of cloth and iron, having now become fully equal to the annual supply, and being at times even in excess of it. That demand, too, was liable at any moment to be increased by the sale in our markets of certificates of debt then held abroad to the extent of hundreds of millions, the proceeds being claimed in gold, and thus causing ruin to the banks. To be out of debt is to be out of danger, but to be in debt abroad to the extent of hundreds of millions is to be always in danger of both public and private bankruptcy. *The control of our whole domestic commerce was therefore entirely in the hands of foreigners who were from hour to hour becoming richer by means of compelling us to remain so dependent upon them that they could always fix the prices at which they would buy the skins, and those at which they would be willing to sell the tails.* As a necessary consequence of this, the nation was not only paralyzed, but in danger of almost immediate death.

Such having been the state of things on the day of Mr. Lincoln's inauguration, let us now look at the remedy that was then required. Let us, for a moment, suppose the existence of an individual with wealth so great that all who knew him might have entire confidence in the performance of what he promised. Let us then suppose that he should have said to the laborers of the country, "Go into the mills, and I will see that your wages are paid;" to the millers, "Employ these people, and I will see that your cloth is sold;" to the farmers, "Give your food to the laborer and your wool to the millers, and I will see that your bills are at once discharged;" to the shopkeepers, "Give your coffee and your sugar to the farmer, and I will see that payment shall forthwith be made;" to the city traders, "Fill the orders of the village shopkeeper and send your bills to me for payment;" to the landlords, "Lease your houses and look to me for the rents;" to all, "I have opened a *clearing house* for the whole country, and have done so with a view to enable every man to find on the instant a cash demand for his labor and its products, and my whole fortune has been pledged for the performance of my engagements;" and then let us examine into the effects. At once the societary circulation would have been restored. Labor would have come into demand, thus doubling at once the productive power of the country. Food would have been demanded, and the farmer would have been enabled to improve his machinery of cultivation. Cloth would have been sold, and the spinner would have added to the number of his spindles. Coal and iron would have found increased demand, and mines and furnaces would have grown in numbers and in size. Houses becoming more productive, new ones would have been built. The *paralysis* would have passed away, life, activity, and energy having taken its place, all these wonderful effects having resulted from the simple pledge of the one sufficient man that he would see the contracts carried out. He had pledged his credit and nothing more.

What is here supposed to have been done is almost precisely what *has* been done by Mr. Lincoln and his Administration, the only difference being, that while in the one case the farmers and laborers had been required to report themselves to the single individual or his agents, the Government has, by the actual purchase of labor and its products, and the grant of its pledges in a variety of shapes and forms, enabled each and every man in the country to arrange his business in the manner that to himself has seemed most advantageous. To the laborer it has said, We need your services, and in return will give you that which will enable your family to purchase food and clothing. To the farmer it has said, We need food, and will give you that by means of which you can pay the shopkeeper. To the manufacturer it has said, We need cloth, and will give you that which will enable you to settle with the workman and the farmer. To the naval constructor it has said, We need your ships, and will give you that which will enable you to purchase timber, iron, and engines. In this manner it is that domestic commerce has been stimulated into life, the result exhibiting itself in the facts, that while we have in the last three years increased to an extent never known before the number of our houses and ships, our mills, mines, and furnaces, our supplies of food, cloth, and iron; and while we have diversified our industry to an extent that is absolutely marvellous; we have been enabled to lend, or pay, to the Government thousands of millions of dollars, where before, under the system which made us wholly dependent on the mercy of the "most wealthy capitalists" of England, we found it difficult to furnish even tens of millions. The whole history of the world presents no case of a financial success so perfect.

In the physical body health is always the accompaniment of rapid circulation, disease that of a languid one. Now, for the first time since the settlement of these colonies, have we had experience of the first. Every man who has desired to work, has found a purchaser for his labor. Every man who has had labor's products to sell, has found a ready market. Every man who has had a house to rent, has found a tenant. And why? Because the Government had done for the whole nation what Companies do for localities when they give them railroads in place of wagon roads. It had so facilitated exchange between consumers and producers, that both parties had been enabled to pay on the instant for all they had had need to purchase.

Important, however, as is all this, it is but a part of the great work that has been accomplished. With every stage of progress there has been a diminution in the general rate of interest, with constant tendency towards equality in the rate paid by the farmers of the East and the West, by the owner of the little workshop and by him who owns the gigantic mill. For the first time in our history the real workingmen—the laborer, the mechanic, and the little village shopkeeper—have been enabled to command the use of the machinery of circulation at a moderate rate of interest. For the first time have nearly all been enabled to make their purchases cash in hand, and to select from among all the dealers those who would supply them cheapest. For the first time has this class known anything approaching to real independence; and therefore has it been that, notwithstanding the demands of the war, capital has so rapidly accumulated. The gain to the working people of the Union thus effected, has been more than the whole money cost of the war, and therefore has it been that all have been able to pay taxes, while so many have been enabled to purchase the securities offered by the Government.

Further than all this, we have for the first time acquired something approaching to a *national independence.* In all time past, the price of money having been wholly dependent on the price in England, the most important intelligence from beyond the Atlantic was that which was to be found in the price of British securities on the Exchange of London. With each arrival, therefore, we were, to our great enlightenment, and that too by means of flaming capitals, informed that Consols had risen or had fallen, our railroad shares then going up or down because the Bank of England had seen fit to purchase a few Exchequer bills, or had found it necessary to part with some of those it previously had held. In all this there has been a change so complete that the price of British Consols has ceased entirely to enter into American calculations. The stride, in this respect alone, that has been made in the direction of independence, is worth to the country more than the whole money cost of the great war in which we are now engaged.

The time had come to make it, the course of Britain having recently been in a direction that limits the circulation and insures a rise in the rate of interest. The Bank of England is limited to £14,000,000 as the amount of notes that may be issued in excess of the gold actually in its vaults. All other banks being limited to the amount that existed on a certain day in 1844, and some of them having since that time gone out of existence, the result exhibits itself in the fact that the total machinery of circulation supplied by the banks is less now than it was twenty years since. As a consequence of this, and in despite of the extraordinary influx of gold from California and Australia, the rate of interest charged for the use of such machinery has been for some years past higher than that paid in any of our Atlantic cities, the fluctuations in regard to paper of the highest character having been between six and ten per cent. By the last accounts it had fallen to 5½, and that is now, as English journalists advise us, as much to be regarded as the normal price of money as was 4 per cent. before the discovery of California mines. The danger of dependence upon the British money market, always great, has now been much increased; and it must become greater with every year, so long as British banking operations shall continue to be governed by that wonderfully absurd system for which the British people stand to-day indebted to the financial ignorance of Sir Robert Peel.

Great and obvious as have been the benefits derived by the country from the system inaugurated under the administration of Mr. Lincoln, they are, as we are assured, counterbalanced by their tendency to produce inflation, and thus to increase the price of gold. How little truth there is in this, I propose to show in another letter, and meanwhile remain, my dear sir,

Very truly and respectfully yours,

HENRY C. CAREY.

Hon. SCHUYLER COLFAX.

PHILADELPHIA, Feb. 13, 1865.

THE CURRENCY QUESTION.

LETTER THIRTEENTH.

DEAR SIR:—

That the currency has been, and is, inflated, is beyond a question. Whence, however, has come the inflation? What has caused the existence of disease? Such are the questions to which an answer must be obtained before we undertake to prescribe the remedy to be adopted. Failing to do this, we shall certainly kill the patient.

By all the currency doctors, both here and abroad, the cause of financial crises is found in the circulation; and hence it has been that both here and elsewhere the world has been furnished with so many laws in regard to it, none of which would ever have existed had the matter been properly understood. To that question it was that Sir Robert Peel addressed himself when he framed a law that has already twice broken down, and that must continue to break down on each successive recurrence of the state of things it was intended to prevent. The statute-books of nearly all of our States present to view similar laws, all of which have proved as utterly worthless, and some of them almost as injurious, as that British one above referred to.

The circulation needs no regulation, and for the simple reason that the people regulate it for themselves. For proof of this, look, I pray you, to the fact that the Treasury has been for several years past engaged in trying to obtain for small notes a circulation amounting to fifty millions, and yet has not, at this hour, one of even the half of that amount. Why has it not? Because the people need no more than twenty or twenty-five millions. If they did need more, they would gladly take it. When Congress had before it a bill authorizing the emission of that description of currency, it would have been deemed rank heresy to say that no limitation was needed, yet has experience proved that such was certainly the case. Had they omitted all restriction on the "greenbacks," they might perhaps have found, as in the case of the smaller notes, that the people understood better what they needed than did their legislators. That they would have done so, I regard as beyond a question.

It is constantly assumed that it is the banks that determine how many notes shall be in use, and yet the experience of each and every individual in the community proves that exactly the reverse of this is true. That you, my dear sir, may satisfy yourself of this, I pray you to look for a moment to your own constant action in regard to the question now before us. On a given day you receive a quantity of bank-notes, which are *then* in circulation. What do you then do with them? You place them in a bank, and thus put them *out of circulation.* On the following day you perhaps take them from the bank and pay them out, thus putting them *again in circulation.* What control did the bank exercise over these several operations? None whatsoever. It is you, your friends, neighbors, and fellow-citizens generally, that regulate the circulation, and it is just as wise to pass laws limiting its amount as it would be to pass other laws determining the quantity of coal, iron, sugar, or coffee to be provided for their use.

To this it is due that in communities that are really independent the circulation is so very nearly a constant quantity. That of the Bank of England, in the eventful period from 1832 to 1841, averaged £18,000,000, and although it embraced the time of one of the greatest excitements and one of the most fearful reverses ever known in that country, the circulation never went beyond that average to the extent of five per cent., nor fell below it to that of eight per cent. The differences exhibited are less even than might be reasonably looked for by any one familiar with the fact that during several of the years every workingman had been fully employed, while in several others a large portion of the manufacturing population was either idle or but half employed.

Take now the following figures representing, in millions, the circulation of the New York banks, and see how uniform was its amount until the withdrawal in 1857, by the banks, of many millions of *loans that had been based upon deposits*, had almost annihilated the commerce of the country, and thus deprived our people of the power to make use of notes.

1855	41	1859	36	1862	42
1856	41	1860	38	1863	42
1057	41	1861	36	1864	40
1858	35				

In every case, as here presented, reduction had been a *consequence* of stoppage of the societary circulation, and *not a cause of it.*

We are told, however, of the depreciation of Continental money, French *assignats*, and Confederate notes, and are threatened that we shall here experience the same result; but those who present such views can scarcely properly appreciate the difference between the conditions under which such paper was emitted and those in which we stand. The first was issued by a Confederation that was little better than a rope of sand, and that had no certain power to provide for the ultimate payment of either principal or interest of any debt it might contract. The second were at first receivable only in payment for confiscated property, and were of no value for any other purpose. As the country became more and more "a scene of rude commotion," and as employment for the people passed away, their quantity was more and more increased, and they then were made a legal tender, but there existed then no organized government capable of giving protection to either property or life—none capable of making secure provision for any ultimate assumption of payment by the State. The last has been issued by an authority the permanent maintenance of which has been so much doubted that few have held its securities longer than was required for enabling them to pass them off to some one else. They have been received by a community that has been cut off from the outer world, and whose single source of wealth has wholly disappeared. They are now used by one whose numbers are constantly diminishing, and over a surface that is becoming daily more and more circumscribed. When the notes were few in number the Southern people were still rich, and, with the exception of Maryland, the notes circulated in every State south of Mason and Dixon's Line, the Ohio and the Missouri. Now, when they so much abound, the rich have become poor, the poor have become poorer, rich and poor to a great extent have passed out of existence, and the theatre of circulation has become limited to portions of half a dozen

States. No one desires to convert Confederate paper into a permanent security, it being clearly obvious that of security for future payment there can be none. The notes will still at some price help to pay for a negro or a horse, but the bonds will not do so at any price whatsoever.

Contrast here, my dear sir, the circumstances above described with those under which our "greenbacks" have been issued. They have gone out in payment for property purchased of, or services rendered by, persons who have freely sold the one or rendered the other. The authority by which they have been issued is one quite as capable of binding posterity as was the Government of Washington and Adams. They are used by a people whose numbers are constantly growing, and whose productive powers are steadily increasing in the ratio which they bear to population. The man who receives them finds himself surrounded by other men who gladly give him houses and lands at prices little greater than those he would have paid ten years since, and before the great free trade crisis of 1857. In all this the Government co-operates by authorizing him to deposit with its officers, for periods long or short, any amount for which he may not have present use, receiving in return certificates by means of which he can withdraw the amount on giving certain notice; or at his pleasure receive bonds payable in three, four, ten, twenty, or forty years, receiving interest in gold or paper, according to the terms agreed upon; and here we have a security against depreciation the like of which the world had never seen before. It is a *safety valve* such as could not have been provided by any of the authorities to which the world has been indebted for those chapters of financial history which are connected with the Continental paper, the Assignat, or the Confederate notes.

Having thus shown what had been the circumstances under which the "greenbacks" have been offered for acceptance by the world, I propose now to show what is the extent to which they have been issued, and what have been the gold phenomena by which that issue has been attended.

The first batch of notes amounted to $60,000,000, and were issued under laws passed in July and August, 1861. Nearly the whole of these have since been withdrawn and cancelled.

The second emission was under a law of February, and the third under one of July, 1862, giving us at the close of that year a total

Government circulation of little less than $300,000,000. The price of gold as yet had changed but slightly. In June, 1862, it still stood at 104. In July and August it fluctuated between 109 and 119. In October it rose to 124, and for the rest of the year it varied between 130 and 137. Compared with what we since have seen, the advance thus far seems as very trifling; and yet the amount of legal tender notes then existing bore a very much *larger proportion* to the number of persons to whom a currency was to be supplied—to the business that was to be transacted—and to the surface that was to be covered than is at this moment borne by the notes now in circulation. Such being the case, as I propose to show it is, we must certainly look elsewhere for the cause of the present price of gold.

In February, 1863, that price rose to 171. Why was this? Not certainly because of any increase in the "greenback" circulation, the further emission of these having been accompanied by the withdrawal of the original $60,000,000 of treasury notes of which but $3,351,000 remained out in the following June. The amount of circulation must, therefore, have been but little more at this time, when gold was at 171, than it had been in the previous autumn when its price ranged between 115 and 124.

In the following month a further issue to the extent of $150,000,000 was authorized, and, according to the generally received theory, gold should now have risen. Did it so? On the contrary it fell, and in July, although the greenbacks then outstanding amounted to $400,000,000, was as low as 124. As it seems to me, we cannot in this direction find the cause of changes such as these.

In September the greenbacks issued had risen to $415,000,000, and the price of gold to 143. The two, however, could have had no necessary connection with each other, gold being now much *lower* than it had been in the previous February, while the circulation was *higher* by little less than $100,000,000.

By the act of March, 1863, the Secretary had been empowered to issue interest-bearing notes, legal tender for their face, to the extent of $400,000,000. Of this power no use appears to have been made prior to the first of October of that year. In that and the following month there were issued of greenbacks $15,000,000, and of interest-bearing legal tenders $35,000,000; and it is fair to assume a further issue for December of $30,000,000, bringing up the total amount to nearly $500,000,000. What was the effect of this upon gold? Did it carry it up to, or beyond, the price at which it had stood in the previous February? On the contrary, although in the meantime $200,000,000 had been added to the legal tenders issued, it remained 20 per cent. lower, the price on the first of January being only 151. How the opponents of what is called "the paper money system" can reconcile these facts, I do not clearly see.

Since then the price has been nearly as follows:—

January	157	May	192	September	220
February	159	June	240	October	220
March	165	July	276	November	230
April	178	August	257	December	220

Throughout the whole of these latter months there had been the most violent fluctuations, but these figures will, I think, suffice to give you, my dear sir, a general idea of the whole movement.

What, in the meantime, had been the course of the Treasury in regard to the issue of legal tender notes? For a reply to this question I must refer you to the following figures exhibiting the state of that portion of the public debt on the first of November last:—

I. Of greenbacks the amount then outstanding was	$433,000,000
II. Of one year notes	43,000,000
III. Of two year notes	16,000,000
IV. Of two year coupon notes	61,000,000
V. Of three year notes	102,000,000
	$655,000,000

The amount is here shown to have been greater by about one hundred and fifty millions than it had been a year before, but of this how much was there that really remained in circulation? At the present moment, as I am assured, two-thirds of Nos. II., III., and IV. have been absorbed by individuals and institutions, and have ceased to constitute any portion of the circulation. Such, likewise, is the case with a portion of No. V. Admitting, now, the quantity since issued of this last to be equal to the amount of the others so absorbed in the last three months, we obtain, as a deduction from the above *apparent* circulation, the large sum of $80,000,000, and thus reduce the real amount to $575,000,000.

Is this, however, all the deduction needed to be made? By no means! Throughout this period banks have been parting with their gold, and substituting for it United States notes, both demand and interest-bearing, and individuals, to a vast extent, have followed their example. The farmer pays for what he needs in local notes, but he puts aside his "greenbacks." The miner and the mechanic—the laborer and the village shopkeeper—the soldier and the sailor—the immigrant who is seeking to invest his little capital, and the sempstress who is trying to accumulate the means with which to purchase a sewing-machine—all of these have become hoarders of "greenbacks," which have thus been withdrawn from circulation, and have, for the time being, no more influence upon either the gold or produce markets than they would have had they been altogether blotted out of existence. Adding now together all these quantities, we shall, as I think, readily obtain the sum of $75,000,000, and thus reduce the actual Treasury circulation to the precise point at which it stood at the close of 1863, when the price of gold was 151.

There is, however, another portion of the circulation which now demands attention. At the date of which I have spoken there were in existence 631 national banks, with an authorized capital of $428,000,000, to which there had been *issued* notes amounting to $72,000,000. To what extent those notes had then been *circulated* we cannot tell, but we know, from the Report of the Commissioner of the Currency, that on the first Monday of the previous October their actual circulation amounted to only $45,260,000, to meet which, and to provide for payment of their depositors, they held, in "specie and other lawful money," $44,801,000. Of the first, the quantity held is likely to have been very small indeed, but admitting it to have been even as much as $10,000,000, and that another sum of equal amount had been in the form of interest-bearing legal tenders, the quantity of "greenbacks" held by them must have been $25,000,000. This would reduce their *apparent* addition to the quantity of "paper money" to but $20,000,000; but when we take into view the fact that in the year embraced in the Report 168 State banks had become national institutions, and that, to the extent of their issues, the new notes had been mere substitutes for those previously in existence, we see that the *real* addition thus made to the circulation had been a quantity too small to be worthy of any serious attention.

At the date of the battle of Gettysburg, say July 3, 1863, the legal tender circulation was, as has been shown, $400,000,000, with gold at 124. With a present circulation of only $500,000,000, gold is above 200; and yet, as I propose now to show, its amount is *very far less*, in proportion to the space over which it is circulated, to the population to be supplied, and to the work to be done, than it was at the date to which I have referred.

At that time we had secure possession of scarcely any portion of the country south of Mason and Dixon's Line, the Ohio and the Missouri. We did, it is true, still hold Washington, but a rebel army was then in Maryland. South of that, in the Atlantic States, we held Fortress Monroe, Norfolk, Newbern, Hilton Head and its immediate neighborhood. Kentucky was then exceedingly disturbed, while Tennessee was mainly occupied by rebel armies. Missouri was, in almost its whole extent, a "debateable land," while rebel forces occupied nearly the whole of Arkansas and by far the larger portion of Louisiana. On the Mississippi we held Memphis at the north and New Orleans at the South. Throughout the border and Southern States, therefore, there was little work being done, and little use for circulation of any description whatsoever; and of what was used nearly the whole consisted of Confederate notes.

To-day, the Federal circulation is needed throughout Maryland, the larger portion of old Virginia, Kentucky, Tennessee, Missouri, Arkansas, much of Mississippi and Louisiana, parts of Georgia, Alabama, and North Carolina, and throughout the whole region bordering on the Mississippi. It is needed, too, by every emigrant to Minnesota, Nebraska, Colorado, and Nevada; and thus, while we have, in the last eighteen months, added largely to the population to be supplied, we have almost doubled the territory within which that population may be found.

Simultaneously with all this we have added little less than one-half to the productive powers of our people, and to the transactions for facilitating which a general medium of circulation is required.

Having studied these things you will, my dear sir, as I think, be disposed to agree with me in the conclusions at which I have arrived, as follows:—

That the circulation bears now a much smaller proportion to the need for it than it did at the time when gold stood at 124.

That to this is to be attributed that the "greenback" is frequently so scarce as to interfere, and that seriously, with the operations of the Government; and

That, if we desire to find the cause of the present high price of gold, it is in quite another direction we must look for it.

What that direction is I propose to show in another letter, and meanwhile remain,

Yours, very truly,

HENRY C. CAREY.

Hon. Schuyler Colfax.

Philadelphia, February 13, 1865.

THE CURRENCY QUESTION.

LETTER FOURTEENTH.

DEAR SIR:—

The power of a bank to make loans is derived from the use of its capital; from its power to furnish circulation; and from its further power to apply to the purchase of securities the moneys standing to the credit of those with whom it deals, and known by the name of *deposits.*

That it is not to the use of the first we are indebted for the inflation now complained of is very certain. That variations in the second have been only those consequent upon changes otherwise produced has been already shown. There remains, then, only the third, and to that it is that I now propose to call your attention, first, however, asking you to accompany me for a moment in an examination of the effect which necessarily results from the loan by banks of moneys for which they themselves are indebted to others, and which they may, at any moment, be called upon to refund.

Let us suppose you, yourself, to have received on any given day notes, or specie, amounting to ten, fifteen, twenty, or fifty thousand dollars, and that while waiting to re-invest them you have placed them in your safe. Going now on change, you find that sum to be there represented by *yourself alone.*

Let us next suppose that instead of so placing them you had had them put to your credit in a neighboring bank, and that the bank had forthwith lent them to a dealer in money, or in stocks. Going on change under these circumstances you find your money *twice represented;* first by yourself who have it, as you suppose, in the bank; and next, by the man who had borrowed it and had had it put to *his* credit precisely as it had previously been placed to *yours.* Here is a very simple operation by means of which the amount of deposits has been doubled *by the action of the bank itself;* and here it is that we find the cause of all the inflation of which we so often have had reason to complain, and to which, as I propose to show, we chiefly owe the numerous and extraordinary changes in the price of gold.

By the last report of the Superintendent of the New York banks the amount for which they then stood indebted to individuals, called depositors, was nearly $250,000,000. The owners of this vast sum might be seen passing up and down Wall Street, as fully ready to purchase stocks or notes as they could have been had it been in their private safes. Side by side with them, however, might be seen other individuals to whom *that same amount* had been lent, and who were equally ready to bid for any securities that might be offered. The $250,000,000 of *capital* had thus become $500,000,000 of *currency*, so to remain until the owners might claim to be repaid. The bank then making the same demand upon its debtors the $500,000,000 of currency would forthwith shrink into its original dimensions, and become once again but $250,000,000.

No such general demand would, of course, ever be made, and that none such has been needed for producing the crises of the past, or the gold excitements of the present, will be seen on an examination of the following figures, presenting, in millions, the movements of the New York banks before and after the great crisis of 1857 :—

	June '56.	Sept. '56.	June '57.	Sept. '57.	Dec. '57.
Capital . . .	92	96	104	107	107
Circulation . .	31	34	32	27	24

Leaving the circulation now wholly unprovided for, we will take the amount of the so-called deposits, and set against these latter the whole amount of specie with a view to ascertain what had been the amount of currency created by *the ballooning system* :—

Deposits . .	103	104	109	85	83
Specie . . .	14	15	14	14	29
Lent out . .	89	89	95	71	54

In the first two of these periods 89 millions of real capital had become 178 of currency. In the third *that* currency had risen to 190. In the last it had, by the simple process of calling in loans, been carried down to 108.

The facts here exhibited in regard to the circulation are—

First, that up to the moment just preceding the explosion there had not only been no increase, but an actual reduction in its amount; second, that that reduction had been *consequent* upon a closing of workshops and suspension of business otherwise produced; and third, that, notwithstanding the almost entire suspension of business, the apparent reduction was but $8,000,000. That the real one must have been very far less than this will be obvious to all who know how large is the amount of notes of other banks remaining unexchanged, and for the time being out of circulation, at a time of financial ease, compared with that which is so retained in a period of crisis as severe as that now under examination.

Those exhibited in regard to the process of *duplication* to which your attention has been called, are as follows:—

First. The very small increase that had been required for producing the largest excitement throughout the country at large. The total amount from June, 1856, to June, 1857, was, as here is shown, but six millions; and yet there had been thus produced an inflation of the value of property throughout the country to the extent of many hundreds of millions:

Second. The very small reduction required for precipitating a whole community into a state of absolute and entire ruin, such as existed at the date of the last returns here given. The whole reduction had been but forty-one millions, and yet the changes in the value of property thereby produced counted certainly by thousands of millions.

What caused the rise? The use *by* banks of the property of others. What caused the fall? The demand *of* the banks for payment by their debtors. Who suffered? Every man who was in debt. Who profited? Every one who had the command of money. The rich were thus made richer and the poor made poorer by means of an inflation caused by the action of those very bank managers who, in all times past, had largely profited of such changes.

With all this, as has been shown, the circulation had nothing whatsoever to do, nor could it have, for the reason that *that* portion of the currency is governed by the people themselves, and not in any manner controlled by bank directors. Nevertheless, all our laws are framed as if the circulation were really the portion which needed regulation.

Following out the view thus presented I give you now, in

the following figures, the movement of the same institutions in the past four years:—

	June '61.	June '62.	Dec. '62.	June '63.	Sept. '63.	Mar. '64.	June '64.	Sept. '64.
Capital	110	109	109	108	109	109	108	107
Circulation	26	39	39	32	33	31	32	33

In the first of these periods the circulation was small because our people were almost wholly unemployed. This was a *consequence* of error elsewhere, and not itself a cause of error.

Deposits and bank balances .	139	206	258	272	288	354	298	297
Specie and bank balances .	60	55	65	63	53	46	43	40
Lent out	79	151	193	209	235	308	255	257

The duplication of these vast sums, consequent upon the very simple process of placing money to the credit of A, as a depositor of his own property, and to that of B as a borrower of the same money, gives the following very remarkable figures:—

	158	302	386	418	470	616	510	514
Price of gold at same dates	par	103 to 109	131 to 133	147	128 to 142	161 to 165	195 to 245	255 to 191

The seventh column gives the precise period of the agitation caused by the passage of *the gold bill;* and from that to the eighth we have in the price of gold the effect of the extreme depression of the public mind of July and August last. It is by no means to be assumed that the gold variations have been altogether caused by the inflation above exhibited; but, that they have to nearly their whole extent been so, the figures above most clearly prove. Were bank loans reduced to the point at which they stood three years since, gold would be now as cheap as it was then.

The *addition* to the currency that had thus been made by the banks of the single State of New York, in comparing March, '64, with June, '61, appears to have been precisely $229,000,000. In all such movements the rest of the country, although at a long distance, follows suit to New York city. Three years since, when gold was still at par, the debts, called deposits, of the Pennsylvania banks, stood at $25,000,000. A year since, with gold at 165, they had already doubled; and since that time the movement in the direction of expansion has been at a greatly accelerated pace. In the last twelve months the deposit line of the Philadelphia banks alone has increased $14,500,000, most of their gold meanwhile having been converted into interest-bearing legal tender notes. As a consequence of all this, the interest-bearing securities held by them are little less than quadruple the amount of their capital. The inflation of this city alone is greater than was that of New York city prior to the great crisis of 1857.

The *addition* thus made to the currency of Pennsylvania can scarcely be estimated at less than $40,000,000. Allowing now for all the rest of the loyal States only twice that sum, we obtain $120,000,000, which, added to that of New York, gives us a total of $349,000,000.

Of what does this addition consist? Of precisely the same material that is used for inflating all other balloons—gas, *and nothing else.* The slightest pinhole causes it to disappear, and therefore is it that we meet with changes in the dimensions of the machine violent as are those here exhibited in figures representing, in millions, the loans, throughout the past year, of New York city banks:—

January . .	174 to 162	July . . .	198 to 185
February . .	163 to 174	August . .	185 to 188
March . .	182 to 199	September . .	189 to 185
April . . .	203 to 194	October . .	185 to 186
May . . .	198 to 195	November . .	187 to 192
June . . .	196 to 197	December . .	196 to 204

At one moment, as we see, gas is injected, and prices of gold, stocks, and commodities generally throughout the country, rise—and then the initiated sell. At another, it is compelled to escape, prices then falling, to the great advantage of those who had so lately sold. Such is the movement that is allowed to remain unregulated, the aid of Congress being meanwhile invoked in favor of establishing control over a circulation already regulated by means of that "higher law" which subjects to the popular will that portion of the financial movement.

Most widely different from all this is the action of that portion of the currency furnished by the Treasury, and known by the popular name of "greenbacks." In the one case, the addition represents nothing but *the will* of certain persons whose interests are to be promoted by expansion, to be followed, on the succeeding day probably, by contraction. In the other, it represents property delivered or service rendered to the Government. In the one, it is local, and the effect upon prices is great in proportion to the limitation of the space. In the other, it is paid out to the soldier, wherever found, whether in the hospitals of New England, the camps of the Centre, or the armies of the South and Southwest. It goes into the pocket of each individual, there to remain until he can find an opportunity to send it home, or in some other manner to use it for his private benefit. It goes into the pockets of farmers, miners, mechanics, laborers, sailors, traders large and small, enabling each and every one to buy for cash, and cheaply, what before he could obtain only at the single shop at which he could have credit. It helps to build ships on the Atlantic and the Pacific, on the lakes, and on the Mississippi; and it pays the men who sail or work those ships. It enters into every home of the Union, and into every old stocking by help of which the sewing-woman is preparing for the purchase of a machine, or the laborer for that of a house. The field of its operation is coextensive with the Union, and its power to affect injuriously the prices of gold, labor, or commodities generally, is in the *inverse ratio* of the extent of that field. Nevertheless, to prevent the possibility of injury from that source, the Treasury has created an acceptable investment, coextensive with the "greenbacks" in amount, by means of which every holder is enabled to convert into an interest-bearing security whatsoever surplus may be in his hands. Having thus provided a perfect *escape-valve*, neither the captain nor the crew need fear explosion.

The banker, on the contrary, desires that there may be no valve whatsoever but that which he himself controls. When it suits him, he injects the gas, and continues so to do until he has arrived as near as he dares to go to the point at which explosion may be looked for. Next he withdraws the gas with equal rapidity, and thus produces crises like that of 1857, the following brief account of which, taken from Gibbons's *Banks of New York*, may now, my dear sir, have some interest for you:—

"The most sagacious of our city bank officers saw no indications of an unusual storm in the commercial skies. When the loans reached the unprecedented height of one hundred and twenty-two millions of dollars, on the eighth of August, they pointed to the annual reduction of ten or twelve millions in the autumn months, as one of the regular ebbs to which the market is subject; but they had no foresight of extraordinary pressure, and no dreams of panic. Credit was extended, but 'the country never was so rich.'

"The banks began to contract their loans about the eighth of August. Securities immediately fell in price at the Stock Board. The failure of a heavy produce house was explained by the depression of that particular interest in the market. A report of dishonest jobbing, and of the misuse of funds in a leading railway company, caused partial excitement, without seriously disturbing confidence in mercantile credit.

"On the twenty-fourth of August, the suspension of the Ohio Life Insurance and Trust Company was announced. It struck on the public mind like a cannon shot. An intense excitement was manifested in all financial circles, in which bank officers participated with unusual sensitiveness and want of self-possession. Flying rumors were exaggerated at every corner. The holders of stock and of commercial paper hurried to the broker, and were eager to make what a week before they would have shunned as a ruinous sacrifice.

"Several stock and money dealers failed, and the daily meetings of the Board of Brokers were characterized by intense excitement.

"Every individual misfortune was announced on the news bulletins in large letters, and attracted a curious crowd, which was constantly fed from the passing throng.

"The Clearing House report for the twenty-ninth of August—the first after the suspension of the Ohio Life Insurance and Trust Company—showed a reduction of four millions of dollars in the bank loans during the previous week.

"The most substantial securities of the market fell rapidly in price at public sale.

"The safety of bank-notes in circulation was suspected or denied. The publishers of counterfeit detectors spread alarm among the shopkeepers and laborers, by selling handbills with lists of broken banks, which were cried about the streets by boys, at 'a penny a-piece.'

"One of the Associated Banks fell into default at the end of August, and a fraud of seventy thousand dollars by the paying teller roused suspicion of similar misconduct in other institutions.

"The regular discount of bills by the banks had mostly been suspended, and the street rates for money, even on unquestionable securities, rose to three, four, and five per cent. a month. On the ordinary securities of merchants, such as promissory notes and bills of exchange, money was not to be had at any rate. House after house of high commercial repute succumbed to the panic, and several heavy banking firms were added to the list of failures.

"The settlements of the Clearing House were watched with the expectation of new defaults; and their successful accomplishment, each day, was a subject of mutual congratulation among bank officers.

"The statement of the city banks for the week ending September 5th showed a further reduction in the loans of more than four millions of dollars.

"Commercial embarrassments and suspension became the chief staple of news in all the papers of town and country. The purchase and transportation of produce almost entirely ceased.

"From this period, there was nothing wanting to aggravate the common distress for money. The failure of the Bank of Pennsylvania, in Philadelphia, was followed by that of the other banks of that city, and by those of Baltimore, and of the Southern Atlantic States generally. Commercial business was everywhere suspended. The avalanche of discredit swept down merchants, bankers, moneyed corporations, and manufacturing companies, without distinction. Old houses, of accumulated capital, which had withstood the violence of all former panics, were prostrated in a day, and when they believed themselves to be perfectly safe against misfortune.

"The bank suspension of New York and New England, in the middle of October, was the climax of this commercial hurricane.

"Such is the outline of the most extraordinary, violent, and destructive financial panic ever experienced in this country. What caused it? To what source or sources can it be traced? Where lies the responsibility of it? What lessons does it teach? What preventives are indicated against the recurrence of similar disaster? These are questions which agitate the public mind, and which ought to be answered, if possible, for our instruction and future guidance."

Seeking an answer to these questions, the author furnishes a full statement of the movement, its result being that of showing, as he says, "beyond cavil, that *the banks*, not the depositors, *took the lead in forcing liquidation.* In the twenty days prior to the 26th of September," as he adds, "the deposits fell off but $341,746, while the resources of the banks were increased $6,694,179."

The men who had taken "the lead" in measures which had prepared for the explosion proved now to be those most active in "forcing liquidation," and thus enabling themselves to purchase, at low prices, stocks, bonds, and real estate which they had sold at high ones. Aided by the large fortunes thus acquired men of the same stamp are this day exercising a power thrice greater than was then exhibited, the tendency of all their measures being in the direction of making the poor poorer and the rich richer than ever before; those of the Treasury, meanwhile, looking in a precisely opposite direction, and tending to lower the rate of interest, while increasing the power over his own actions exercised by the laborer, the miner, the mechanic, and the farmer.

The "greenback" has fallen on the country as the dew falls, bringing with it good to all and doing injury to none. The gas-formed currency, on the contrary, is in the financial world what the water-spout is in the natural one. Whirled about by the wind, and wholly uncertain in its movements, none can predict of this latter when or where its effects will most be felt, and all around are therefore kept in a state of fever closely resembling that which distinguishes the financial action of the present hour. The deluge comes at last, destroying both property and life, and making a desert where all before had been happiness and peace.

It is to restrictions upon the formation of the dew that we are now invited, leaving wholly unchecked the action of those who profit of the desolation caused by the water-spout. What are the results that seem to me likely to be obtained as a consequence of acceptance of the invitation, I propose to show in another letter, and meanwhile remain, my dear sir,

Yours, very truly,

HENRY C. CAREY.

Hon. Schuyler Colfax.

Philadelphia, Feb. 15, 1865.

THE CURRENCY QUESTION.

LETTER FIFTEENTH.

DEAR SIR:—

The lugubrious predictions of the London *Times* have, thus far, not been verified. The war is now, to all appearance, coming rapidly to a close, and not only are we not yet ruined, but there prevails throughout the country a prosperity such as, until recently, had never before been known. To what causes may this properly be attributed? How has it been possible that a community should have furnished so many hundreds of thousands of men, and so many thousands of millions of the material of war, without becoming even poorer than before? Let us see.

The act of secession *by* the South was an act of emancipation *for* the North. Up to that date the latter had been mere colonies, governed by those " wealthy British capitalists" whose mode of action is so well described in the Parliamentary Report, an extract from which has already more than once been given, but here repeated because of its powerful bearing on the question now before us:—

"The laboring classes generally, in the manufacturing districts of this country, and especially in the iron and coal districts, are very little aware of the extent to which they are often indebted for their being employed at all to the immense *losses* which their employers voluntarily incur, in bad times, in order *to destroy foreign competition, and to gain and keep possession of foreign markets.* Authentic instances are well known of employers having in such times carried on their works at a loss amounting in the aggregate to three or four hundred thousand pounds in the course of three or four years. If the efforts of those who encourage the combinations to restrict the amount of labor and to produce strikes were to be successful for any length of time, the great accumulations of capital could no longer be made *which enable a few of the most wealthy capitalists to overwhelm all foreign competition in times of great depression*, and thus to clear the way for the *whole trade* to step in when prices revive, and to carry on a great business before *foreign* capital can again accumulate to such an extent as to be able to establish a competition in prices with any chance of success. *The large capitals of this country are the great instruments of warfare against the competing capital of foreign countries*, and are *the most essential* instruments now remaining by which our manufacturing supremacy can be maintained; the other elements—cheap labor, abundance of raw material, means of communication, and skilled labor—being rapidly in process of being equalized."

Profiting of its liberty, the North at once determined on the adoption of measures of protection to the farmer in his efforts for bringing the consumer of his products to take his place in the immediate neighborhood of the place of production, and thus to relieve him from the oppressive tax of transportation imposed upon him by the system above so well described. The effect of this now exhibits itself in the facts—

That the development of our mineral resources has been great beyond all former example:

That diversification in the pursuits of our people now exhibits itself in the naturalization of many of the minor branches of industry in regard to which we had before been wholly dependent upon Europe:

That the demand for labor has been so great as to cause large increase of wages:

That the high price of labor has caused great increase of immigration:

That demand for the farmer's products has so largely increased as to have almost altogether freed him from dependence on the uncertain markets of Europe:

That the internal commerce has so largely grown as to have doubled in its money value the many hundreds of millions of railroad stock:

That the prosperity of existing railroads has caused large increase in the number and the extent of roads:

That here, for the first time in the history of the world, has been exhibited a community in which every man who had labor to sell could sell it if he would, while every man who had coal, iron, food, or cloth to sell could find at once a person able and willing to buy and pay for it:

That, for the first time, too, in the history of the world, there has been presented a community in which nearly all business was done for cash, and in which debt had scarcely an existence:

That, as a necessary consequence of this, there has been a large and general diminution of the rate of interest:

That farmers, laborers, miners, and traders have therefore become more independent of the capitalist, while the country at large has become more independent of the "wealthy capitalists" of Europe:

That, so great have been the economies of labor and its products, resulting from great rapidity of the societary circulation, that, while building more houses and mills, constructing more roads, erecting more machinery, and living better than ever before, our people have been enabled to contribute, in the form of taxes and loans, no less a sum than three thousand millions of dollars to the support of government.

These are wonderful results, and for them we have been largely, yet not wholly, indebted to the re-adoption of the protective system. That alone was capable of doing much, but we should have failed in the prosecution of the war had not the Treasury, by the establishment of a general medium of circulation, given us what has proved to be a great *clearing house*, to which were brought labor and all of labor's products to be exchanged. Increased rapidity of circulation was a necessary consequence of this, and to that increase the greatly improved health of the societary body has been wholly due.

Such having been the results of the two great measures by which the first period of Mr. Lincoln's administration had been distinguished, it might have been believed that neither one of them would be abandoned without at least a full and fair inquiry into the probable consequences of any changes that might be suggested. Those who might have so thought could scarcely, however, have reflected upon the general character of our legislation. "No people," as it has been said, "so soon forget yesterday." None take so little thought of to-morrow. No one looks back to study the cause of the good or evil that exists, and it is as a consequence of this that we have so constantly relapsed into British free trade almost at the first moment that protection had brought about a cure of the evils of which it had been the cause. Hitherto, since 1861, our course has been onward, and in the direction that above is indicated. Now, as I propose to show, we are steadily retracing our steps; and if the forward movement has led us to our present prosperous state, it can scarcely well be doubted that the backward one will lead us once again to that calamitous one from which we so recently have emerged.

The most serious move in the retrograde direction is that one we find in the determination to prohibit the further issue of that circulation to which we have been so much indebted. Why is it made? Because journalists fancy that it is to "paper money" they must attribute the, to them, great fact that paper is so high! Because men who depend on fixed incomes fancy that they should live better were the gold standard once again adopted! Because every free-trader in the land charges the high price of gold to the use of "greenbacks," and sees therein the causes why he cannot, with profit to himself, fill our markets with British cloth and British iron!

What is the present effect of the hesitation of the Treasury to use the power that yet remains at its command? It is paralyzing the societary movement, to the great loss of both the people and the Government. Labor is less in demand. Cloth, iron, and a thousand other commodities move more slowly. Why all these things? Because the Treasury does not fulfil its contracts. The unpaid requisitions amount to $125,000,000, and the Treasury is empty. The contractor who obtains a certificate sells it at heavy loss; while many, as I am told, find difficulties interposed in the way of obtaining certificates, most of which have their origin in the indisposition to *acknowledge* debt when there exist no means with which to *pay* it. How it is with the men who are now serving in the field was well shown, a few days since, by Senator Wilson, when he told his brother Senators that "they needed more money than they could obtain to pay their just debts—what they had agreed to pay." "Tens of millions of dollars," he continued, "are now due to our armies, many of whose officers have been unpaid for months; the Generals, meanwhile, holding by handfuls resignations tendered by men who find themselves forced to retire, as the only means now left to them of providing for their families."

Turning now to a letter in this day's *Tribune*, I find a statement of the facts of the case, and their effects, to which you may perhaps excuse me for asking your attention. It is as follows:—

"It is useless to deny the fact that men once ardent in the cause are becoming lukewarm in their attachment to a Government which so sadly fails to discharge, in this respect, its self-imposed obligations, and seems so careless of those over whom specially the ægis of its protection should be thrown. No wonder that the soldier should grow weary when he reflects that his arduous hardships, undergone on long marches, in the trenches, on the picket line, scorching then under the rays of a midsummer's sun, and shivering now in the merciless blasts of winter, exposed to all the inclemencies of a variable climate, are suffered to go so long unrecognized by his Government; no wonder that when every mail brings him the old story of his family's destitution, and when he remembers his inability to aid them, he should grow lukewarm in the cause which years ago he espoused with all the ardor of a man and a patriot. It is in vain that he tries to place country above home—above the wife whom he has solemnly sworn to cherish and protect, the offspring whom Heaven has given him to support, or the aged parents whose infirmities demand his filial consideration; the thought of his domestic responsibilities will absorb all others, and will embitter every hour of his soldier-life.

"Every day resignations are forwarded by officers whom stern necessity has compelled to ask for their discharge from the military service, in order that they may return home to relieve the pressing wants of their families, and shall we say, too, that desertions to the enemy frequently occur whenever men are impelled by the same motives. Officers and men, in making application for leaves and furloughs, are often forced to make the humiliating confession that they desire to go home to restore order to their households, upon which, during their absence, shame and dishonor have fallen, and the plea of their families' extreme destitution is still more frequent. In the name of humanity, then, let the troops be paid with as little delay as possible; the best interests of the service demand it."

Entirely in keeping with this are statements coming from the West, of the great distress of Government contractors compelled to forced sales of the vouchers in their hands—of the great rise in the general rate of interest—and of the extremely sluggish state of the societary circulation. The Government has made itself responsible for the financial movement of the country, and when it stops payment there is stoppage everywhere.

Why has it stopped? Because those in the control of public journals fail to see that the cause of the high price of paper and of gold *cannot* be found in the circulation! Because the Government itself fails to see that the circulation now furnished bears a smaller proportion to the needs of the people, and to the extent of country requiring to be supplied, than did that which was furnished when gold could be bought at an advance of 10, 12, or 15 per cent.! Because all who write or speak on this subject fail to see that, with the extension of the power of the Union over the Cotton States, there must arise an absolute necessity for furnishing to the people of those States machinery of circulation adequate to the performance of the same work that has so well been done in these

Northern States! So far from diminishing the supply of that machinery, there is a pressing necessity for its increase.

Anxious for a reduction in the price of gold, journalists are almost everywhere calling upon Congress to increase the taxes, to give up *selling* machinery of circulation that costs it nothing, and to take to *buying* such machinery at the market price. Obedient to their orders the treasury *is* buying it, and the price at which it buys is shown in the following extract from an advertisement of the loan that is now on sale:—

> "By authority of the Secretary of the Treasury, the undersigned has assumed the general subscription agency for the sale of United States treasury notes bearing seven and three-tenths per cent. interest per annum, known as the SEVEN-THIRTY LOAN. These notes are issued under date of August 15, 1864, and are payable three years from that time, in currency, or are convertible at the option of the holder into U. S. 5-20 SIX PER CENT. GOLD-BEARING BONDS. These bonds are now worth a premium of nine per cent., including gold interest from November, which makes the actual profit on the 7-30 loan, at current rates, including interest, about ten per cent. per annum, besides its *exemption from State and municipal taxation, which adds from one to three per cent. more*, according to the rates levied on other property."

This is certainly a high price to pay for the use of a little money, and the reason why it is so high is that the supply of the commodity needed is diminishing in the proportion borne by it to public and private needs.

We have here, however, only $200,000,000, interest upon which is to be paid in gold three years hence. Six hundred millions more are now asked for, and the demand is, we are told, to be accompanied by a withdrawal of even the existing power to furnish legal tenders bearing interest. As those now existing become more and more withdrawn from circulation, the societary machinery must gradually diminish in its quantity, and that, too, just at the time when the theatre on which it is to be employed is likely to be almost doubled. The necessary consequence of this must be such a rise in the rate of interest as will compel the export of Government bonds, and the rapid increase of dependence on the money markets of Europe—each step backward being thus but the precursor of another and greater one. So long as they shall continue to be sold abroad money will continue to be obtainable; but when the foreign market shall have become fully glutted it will, as in the period from 1837 to 1842, become unobtainable at any price.

The gold interest now payable requires $60,000,000. Adding these new loans, and making their interest payable in gold, we shall, three years hence, need $108,000,000, most of which is likely to have to go to Europe. Add now to this, first, the $30,000,000 required for payment of interest on the old foreign free trade debt; second, only an equal amount for absentees, temporary and permanent; and we obtain a demand amounting to $168,000,000, that *must* be met before we can purchase a piece of cloth or a ton of iron. Where is all this gold to come from?

Tax the people! is the answer. Give us an income tax of 25 per cent.! Tax sales! Tax manufactures! All this is being done, and so thoroughly that important branches of manufacture are likely to be taxed entirely out of existence. Paying his taxes in paper, and obtaining cash for his products, the ironmaster can scarcely even to-day make head against those "wealthy capitalists" of England who have already placed themselves on such a footing, as regards freight and duty, that it is *they* who, under a gold system, will be protected, and not their American competitors. So, too, with paper, the domestic taxes on which are ten per cent., while foreign paper is likely to be admitted at three. So, too, as I understand, is it with leather. Mr. Sherman tells us that $40,000,000 in gold will be required to purchase paper abroad that if made at home would yield $10,000,000 to the treasury. Add to this $100,000,000 to pay for the iron needed for taking the place of that now made in furnaces that will then be out of blast, and we shall have quite enough to pay to those European nations whose markets are now glutted with food, and who have taken from us, in the past five months, of flour, wheat, and corn, just as much, *and no more*, as would command in gold somewhat less than *two millions of dollars.**

The contributions to the internal revenue made by paper, iron, and leather, appear, under the retrograde system now inaugurated, likely to be very small indeed. How will it be with other manufactures, paying as they must, at a gold value, duties that had been laid when two dollars in paper had been but the equivalent of one

* The precise quantities of these commodities shipped to Belgium, France, and Britain, has been: Of flour, 59,998 barrels; of wheat, 1,305,313 bushels; and of corn, 56,933 bushels.

in gold? How will it be with the farmer, obliged to look to Europe for a market for his products? How will it be with the miner and the laborer when rolling-mills are closed and mines have ceased to be worked? The answer to all these questions will be found in the simple propositions, that the power of accumulation increases almost geometrically as the rapidity of the *societary circulation* increases arithmetically; and that it declines in the same proportion as the circulation becomes more languid. In the few years through which we just have passed it has been increasing rapidly, but, under the change of policy that has been now inaugurated, it is already slowly moving in the opposite direction. Admitting the truth of those propositions, then must it be also admitted that, prompted by an anxious desire once again to handle gold, we are killing the goose that has already laid the many golden eggs so well described in the following paragraph, from this day's *Tribune*:—

"The internal revenue for the month of January just past amounted to the enormous sum of $31,076,902 89—over a million of dollars a day, including Sunday! And yet confessedly the machinery for collecting this branch of the nation's income is imperfect and undergoing change. Vast as is that sum of internal revenue, daily and monthly, how light a burden is it to the business of this rich and vigorous nation! And with what patriotic cheerfulness and acquiescence the people pay this tax to preserve their nation and to maintain democracy."

To what do we owe these wonderful results of a state of civil war? To rapidity of the societary circulation, and to nothing else! To what have we been indebted for that rapidity? To protection and the "greenbacks"! What is it that we are now laboring to destroy? Protection and the Greenback!

Let us continue on in the direction in which we now are moving, and we shall ere long see, not resumption but repudiation; not a contradiction but a confirmation of the predictions of the *Times*; not a re-establishment of the Union, but a complete and final disruption of it.

What are the means by which these calamities may be avoided, I propose to show in another and final letter, and meanwhile remain, my dear sir,

Yours, very truly,

HENRY C. CAREY.

Hon. Schuyler Colfax.

Philadelphia, February 17, 1865.

THE CURRENCY QUESTION.

LETTER SIXTEENTH.

DEAR SIR:—

The measures now in preparation, as regards both the customs and internal revenues, tend, as it appears to me, in the direction of stoppage of the societary circulation, of rise in the rate of interest, of increase in the power of men engaged in the creation of financial water-spouts, and of permanent maintenance of a premium on the precious metals. If so, then, if we are ever again to witness here the regular redemption of promises to furnish gold and silver, it must occur as a consequence of the adoption of a course of policy directly the reverse of all that recently has been done, and all that, if we are to credit the public journals, is in the contemplation of those who are charged with the direction of our financial movements.

The existing derangement of the currency is wholly due to the action of those who manage *the windbag system* described in a former letter, and while their operations shall continue to be, as now they are, wholly unrestrained, financial crises must continue to reappear, and the price of gold must continue to be as uncertain as is their course of action. Such being the case, it is of high importance that proper checks be forthwith instituted, and now, for the first time in our history, is it in the power of Congress to let us have them. To that end, let us have a law declaring—

First, that no bank shall hereafter so extend its investments as to hold in any form other than those of gold, silver, U. S. notes, or notes of national banks, more than twice its capital:

Second, that in the case of already existing banks whose investments are outside of the limits above described, any extension thereof beyond the amount at which they stood on the first of the present month shall be followed by instant forfeiture of its charter.

Having thus established a check upon further extension, the

next step should be in the direction of bringing the operations of existing banks within proper limits. To that end, let us have a provision imposing on all investments outside of the limits above described a tax which, when added to that already existing, shall amount for the present year to one per cent. In the second year let it be made $1\frac{1}{4}$ per cent. on all over 90 per cent. in excess of the actual capital upon which dividends are paid. In the third, $1\frac{1}{2}$ per cent. over 80 per cent.; and in the fourth, $1\frac{3}{4}$ over 70 per cent. Thenceforth let the tax grow at the rate of a quarter per cent. per annum until, by degrees, all banks shall have so enlarged their capitals, or so reduced their loans, as to free themselves from its further payment.

Holding interest-paying securities 70 per cent. in excess of its capital, a bank would be always in a condition of perfect safety, and could give to its stockholders dividends of at least 8 per cent. Such stock would be preferable to almost any other securities in the market, and there would be no difficulty in so enlarging the foundation as to give to the whole structure the form of a true pyramid, instead of the inverted one which now presents itself to the eye of all observers.

Let us have a law embracing these provisions, and we shall then be fairly on the way towards the establishment of a financial system the most perfect the world has ever seen. Let us have it, and, as you will clearly see, the need for restrictions on the circulation will wholly have passed away. The day, indeed, will then be near at hand when banks will have ceased to be competitors with the Treasury for furnishing circulating notes of any kind, and when the nation may profit to the extent of 50, if not even 60 millions a year of the power to furnish the machinery of circulation.

Simultaneously with the passage of such a law, let the Government determine honestly to pay its debts. The soldier in the field, and the officer who is placing his life in daily hazard, have a right to demand of the Treasury that it shall give them such certificates of its indebtedness as will enable their wives and children to go to the neighboring shop and purchase food and clothing.* The contractor and the shipbuilder have a right to claim that when certificates are issued they shall be in such a form as will enable them to

* The amount now due to the army alone is stated by Senator Wilson at the enormous sum of one hundred and thirty-eight millions of dollars.

avoid the further payment of the usurious interest to which they have so long been subjected. Paying promptly, the Government will buy cheaply; and should such payment have the effect of causing the supply of "greenbacks" to be in excess of the demand, the Treasury will thence derive a double benefit: first, in being thus enabled to borrow what it needs at reasonable rates; and second, in having its need for borrowing diminished by reason of the increased stimulus thereby given to that societary circulation upon the rapidity of which it is dependent for both the maintenance and the growth of the Internal Revenue.

The whole South now requires reorganization, and one of the first steps in that direction should be found in furnishing machinery of circulation. As much in need of this stands the whole of that great West for the development of whose wonderful powers we are now exporting in that direction so many hundreds of thousands of our people. If the Government does not supply that machinery, who is there that can or will do so? Look carefully, I pray you, my dear sir, at the vast field that is to be occupied, and at the great work that is to be done, and then wonder with me that the Government should permit its soldiers to perish in the field, while it is debating the terms of a loan to be made to it by men all of whose interests are to be promoted by a diminution of the circulation and an increase of the rate of interest. Let our soldiers be paid, let the credit of the Government be once again re-established, let the rate of interest be kept down, and let the Treasury reassert its independence, and all will yet go well.

Having thus, as paymaster, re-established its credit, let it next place itself in a creditable position as regards those who had been led to see in the Morrill Tariff a pledge of protection against those "wealthy capitalists" whose fortunes count by millions, and who use those millions as "instruments of warfare" by means of which they are enabled to "overwhelm all foreign competition, and to gain and keep possession of foreign markets." Let it restore those great fundamental branches of industry which constitute the pillars of our national temple to the position in which they stood in 1861, increasing the duties on foreign products by just so much as the taxes since imposed on domestic ones, and the result will then exhibit itself in the fact that sugar, tea, coffee, soda ash, and other raw materials of food and manufacture, will twice over make amends for any loss that may be experienced by the revenue be-

11

cause of the substitution of domestic cloth or iron for that now made in foreign furnaces or on foreign looms.

Let these things be done, and we shall then cease to look abroad for purchasers of our bonds. Let this be done, and we shall soon find ourselves on the road towards becoming purchasers of those now held abroad, *every one of which should be redeemed before we ever again place ourselves in a position to be required to furnish gold and silver in payment of our notes.*

To many it might seem that this would be a postponement of resumption to a date so distant that none of them would live to see it. Let, however, all such persons study what was done in this respect in the brief period of the existence of the tariffs of 1828 and 1842; let them next look to what has been done in the past four years; and they will see that all that I have indicated as what is needed to be done, is only what, under a sound and permanent system, *may be done before the lapse of the next decade.*

As a rule, reformers desire to move too rapidly, and therefore fail to attain their objects. They omit to see that when Nature has important purposes to accomplish, she works slowly and with almost invisible machinery, as when she sends the daily morning dew. When she desires merely to destroy a ship or to root up a forest, she sends the tornado or the water-spout. Let us follow her example. We have a great work to accomplish, and we should now profit of the lesson read to the world in that period which followed the close of the great war of the French Revolution, and exhibited a scene of destruction that had never before, in time of peace, been witnessed. Believing it to be one that should be carefully studied, I now invite you, my dear sir, to accompany me in a brief review of the facts in the order of their occurrence.

For twenty years the Bank of England had been injecting gas into the currency, but with the return of peace it became necessary that it should be steadily withdrawn. In the two years from 1815 to 1817, the bank directors had, by means of the very simple operation of calling in its claims on one hand, and reducing its liabilities on the other, reduced the apparent quantity of money at the command of the community to the extent of £12,000,000, or little short of $60,000,000. So far as regarded the operations of society, this had been equivalent to a total annihilation of that large sum, and to that extent a contraction of the standard by which the community was required to measure the value of all other commodities and things. Had the yardstick been doubled in length, or the pound in weight, for the benefit of all persons who had contracted to purchase cloth or corn, the injury inflicted would have been trivial by comparison with the change that was thus effected. As compared with the property of the people of Great Britain, that sum was utterly insignificant, yet did its abstraction cause an arrest of the circulation almost as complete as would be that produced in the physical body by stoppage of the supply of food. Farmers and merchants were everywhere ruined. Of the country banks, no less than two hundred and forty—being one in four of their whole number—stopped payment; while one in ten and a half became actually bankrupt. "Thousands upon thousands," says Mr. McCulloch, "who had in 1812 considered themselves affluent, found they were destitute of all real property, and sunk, as if by enchantment, and without any fault of their own, into the abyss of poverty." Throughout the country, there was, to use the words of Mr. Francis Horner, "an universality of wretchedness and misery which had never been equalled, except perhaps by the breaking up of the Mississippi Scheme in France." *In the midst of all this ruin, however, the bank, which had supplied the gas, prospered more than ever, for the destruction of private credit rendered its vaults and its notes more necessary to the community.*

The groundwork having thus been laid by the bank, Parliament passed, in 1819, an act providing for the resumption of specie payments, and thus re-established, as the law of the land, the standard that had existed in 1797—among the most remarkable measures of confiscation to be found in the annals of legislation. For more than twenty years all the transactions of the United Kingdom had been based upon a currency less in value than that which had existed in 1796. In the course of that long period, land had been sold, mortgages given, settlements made, and other contracts of a permanent nature entered into, to the extent of thousands of millions of pounds, the terms of all of which were now to be changed for the benefit of the receivers of fixed incomes, and to the loss of those who had land, labor, or the produce of either, to sell. As a necessary consequence, land fell exceedingly in price, and mortgagees everywhere entered into possession. Labor became superabundant, and the laborer suffered for want of food. Machinery of every kind was thrown out of use, and manufacturers were ruined. Manufactures, being in excess of the demand, were forced upon foreign markets, to the ruin of the capitalists and workmen, miners and machinists, of the other countries of the world.

Peace had brought with it widespread ruin, but it everywhere enriched the money-lender—*his* commodity rising, while land became so cheap that he could purchase at less than half its previous price. The annuitant and office-holder profited—their dividends and salaries having become payable in coin, that would purchase double the quantity of food and clothing for which they had at first contracted. Farmers and laborers, mechanics and merchants, were impoverished—their taxes remaining unchanged, while their labor, and its products, commanded less than half the money for which they would before have sold.

Bad as is this, it will be *infinitely* worse with us if we shall attempt to follow the example here placed before us. Let us put our house in order; let us adopt the measures needed for making the Declaration of Independence something more than a mere word of small significance; let us do all this slowly and quietly, and we shall set to the world an example in peace even more remarkable than that which has been set in the course of the present extraordinary war—returning to the old standard, and without the occurrence of the slightest crisis.

That this may be done, it is needed only that those who direct our fiscal operations shall recollect that the National Treasury has now become a partner in, and entitled to the lion's share of, the profits of every mine, every furnace, every mill, every workshop, and every farm in the land, and that every increase in the prosperity of such works must be to it a source of double profit: first, that arising out of the direct contributions of the work itself; and second, that resulting from the increased consumption of sugar, tea, coffee, and other commodities consumed by those who mine the coal, roll the iron, and make the engines and the cloth. The day for a clear perception of the existence of this harmony of all real interests may or may not be near at hand. For the promotion of its arrival, we need to see extended throughout the Union the same principle of association that has proved to be so effective throughout the present war. We need to see A GREAT NATIONAL LEAGUE, embracing men who grow wool, and others who convert it into cloth; men who make iron, and others who need railroad bars; men who raise food, and others who combine food and ore into iron; men who build ships, and others who consume the sugar and the tea that ships transport; and finally, men who pay taxes, and others who make the laws under which those taxes are collected. In the words of Jackson, we need to be *Americanized.* Whenever the day shall arrive when we shall have so become, then, and not till then, shall we have placed ourselves in a position successfully to contend for the control of the commerce of the world, and thus to

OUTDO ENGLAND WITHOUT FIGHTING HER.

That control will find its place among the hands and heads of the community that makes and uses the largest quantity of iron. A single decade of the system above described would suffice for placing us, in this respect, side by side with England. At the close of another, she would be left far behind, and we should then have vindicated our claim to that position in the world of which our people so often talk, and of the true means of obtaining which they so little think.

Hoping that the event may prove that the time for serious thought has now really arrived, and begging you to excuse my numerous trespasses on your attention, I remain, my dear sir, with great regard and respect,

Yours, faithfully,

HENRY C. CAREY.

Hon. SCHUYLER COLFAX.

PHILADELPHIA, February 18, 1865.

www.ingramcontent.com/pod-product-compliance
Lightning Source LLC
LaVergne TN
LVHW021400110826
845150LV00007B/1725

9781425513429